'This is a wonderful devotional b special Psalms of Ascents. I personally all along the way, as this journey upwards in the spir enjoy the refreshment that these meditations bring.'
Dr Richard S Hess, Distinguished Professor of Old Testament and Semitic Languages, Denver Seminary, Colorado

'Rob's love of the Psalms leaps off every page of this book in a way that draws us into the profound depth and richness of our Lord's faithfulness and grace in every changing scene of life. This book is food for the soul.'
Rt Rev Mark Tanner, Bishop of Chester

'This is a truly encouraging treatment of the Psalms of Ascents, and provides plenty of useful material for Christian preachers and teachers as well as profound spiritual nourishment for pilgrims. Writing with a clear, accessible style, Rob Shimwell draws on his personal experience as a much-loved pastor to relate these Psalms on the one hand to the life of Jesus, and on the other hand to our struggles and joys as Jesus' disciples. Like the psalmist, he combines realism about suffering, pain, questioning and temptation with abundant hope in a God of unfailing mercy and loving-kindness. He also shows how the longings of the psalmist are fulfilled in Jesus' redeeming work, and makes illuminating connections between events in the Old Testament and the Gospels. I commend this book most warmly as a source of inspiration and guidance "along the way".'
Rt Rev James Newcome, Bishop of Carlisle

'Imaginative, warm, insightful – Rob Shimwell draws upon a lifetime of pastoral ministry in these clever expositions of the pilgrimage Psalms of Ascents, imagining them first on Jesus' lips and then drawing them forward for us today. This is Bible exposition at its best. You will be informed, encouraged and drawn closer to Jesus through this book – read and be blessed!'

Rev Dr Steve Motyer, formerly New Testament lecturer, London School of Theology; Theology and Counselling Programme Leader

PILGRIMAGE & PROMISE

A Journey with Jesus Through the Psalms of Ascents

Rob Shimwell

instant
apostle

First published in Great Britain in 2023

Instant Apostle
104A The Drive
Rickmansworth
Herts
WD3 4DU

British Library Cataloguing-in-Publication Data

A catalogue record for this book is available from the British Library.

This book and all other Instant Apostle books are available from Instant Apostle:

Website: www.instantapostle.com

Email: info@instantapostle.com

ISBN 978-1-912726-72-1

Printed in Great Britain.

Dedication

For my wife and fellow pilgrim, Diana, who has walked every step of the way with me for nearly fifty years, through every valley and over every mountaintop. There could be no better companion!

And for our grandchildren: Jacob, Ella, Thomas, Daniel, Rachel, Callum and Magnus, with our prayers that they will journey throughout their lives with the Lord Jesus.

Thanks

I could not have written these chapters without the help of Glynn Jones, Emil Shehadah, Ruth Lawrence and Annie Garden, who between them have answered my questions, read draft chapters and helped with their suggestions. And extra thanks to Di, who has been so thorough as she read, corrected and commented on my first drafts and lovingly patient when I have disappeared into my study for hours at a time!

The team at Instant Apostle has been a wonderful support every step of the way, offering suggestions, corrections, help, ideas and encouragement. Thank you, everyone!

I want to acknowledge also the encouragement I received from Alec Motyer shortly before he went to be with the Lord. I discussed the idea for this book with him and he insisted that I should start writing! Thank you, Alec.

Contents

Introduction 13

1. Psalm 120: Far From Home 18

2. Psalm 121: Dangerous Journey 30

3. Psalm 122: Jerusalem in Sight! 43

4. Psalm 123: Walking in Dark Valleys 57

5. Psalm 124: Godly Remembrance 68

6. Psalm 125: Praying for Steadfastness 81

7. Psalm 126: Laughter and Tears 93

Reading Psalms 127 and 128 111

8. Psalm 127: Futility and Happiness (The first of two Wisdom Psalms) 115

9. Psalm 128: The Fear of the Lord (The second of two Wisdom Psalms) 124

10. Psalm 129: Oppressed and Wounded 137

11. Psalm 130: Crying From the Depths 146

12. Psalm 131: Learning to Trust 158

13. Psalm 132: Praying on a Grand Scale 171

14. Psalm 133: Relationships on the Journey 185

15. Psalm 134: Arrival! 199

Postscript 208

Introduction

Lord of the cloud and fire,
I am a stranger, with a stranger's indifference;
My hands hold a pilgrim's staff,
My march is Zionward,
My eyes are towards the coming of the Lord,
My heart is in thy hands without reserve.[1]

Some years ago, I walked with a close friend across the Swiss Alps from Chamonix to Zermatt. By day, we travelled along steep and sometimes dangerous paths with breathtaking views. By night, we enjoyed the hospitality of alpine huts and inns, with excellent food and comfortable beds. Each night, I read from a few pages torn from a scruffy paperback of the Psalms. Those pages consisted of Psalms 120-134, the Psalms of Ascents written for pilgrims on a journey. I still have them, yellowed, dog-eared and covered with almost illegible notes!

Since those unforgettable days of walking and companionship, I have lived with those psalms, praying them, studying them, preaching them and, hopefully, living them. They are psalms for every occasion and every situation. They restore faith, bringing light into dark

[1] Arthur Bennett, *The Valley of Vision: a collection of Puritan Prayers and Devotions* (Edinburgh, Banner of Truth Trust, 1975), p108.

places, security when fearful, guidance when wandering and a constantly renewed trust in our covenant-making, promise-keeping, never-changing Lord who walks with us every day of our earthly pilgrimage.

I trust that I can communicate my love for these ancient songs in the chapters that follow. First, though, a few words of introduction are necessary!

Introducing the Psalms of Ascents

So many aspects of the struggles and joys of our lives and faith are covered in these psalms.

Psalm 120 is the prayer of an exile, struggling to live in a country and culture far removed from his homeland. Psalm 121 is as if two pilgrims are walking together, encouraging each other to find safety in their Lord in whom they trust as they face dangers and exhaustion on their journey. Psalm 122 is a song of rejoicing as the pilgrims reach Jerusalem, their destination. The city's virtues are extolled and prayer is made for Jerusalem's peace.

Five of these psalms (123, 124, 129, 130, 131) face up to the struggles of faith under severe trials and suffering.[2] Three others (127, 128, 133) are about our relationships. They speak of the encouragement and blessings that are to be found in our fellow-pilgrims, vital at every stage of our Christian journeys together. We were never meant to

---

[2] Psalm 123 is about ridicule and contempt; Psalm 124 is about situations of fear and danger; Psalm 129 deals with the pain of physical suffering; Psalm 130 describes the dark times we suffer and Psalm 131 will help when we doubt the goodness of God.

travel or suffer alone through a dangerous and threatening world.

Two other psalms (125, 126) are prayers shot through with hope. The city of God is our ultimate destination and, in spite of the dangers, we are to walk in trust with our eyes set firmly on our destination rather than looking downwards at the difficulty of the terrain we tread.

Psalm 132 is the longest of the Psalms of Ascents, encouraging prayer on a grand scale as we remember, affirm and celebrate the promises and purposes of our Lord in time and eternity!

Finally, Psalm 134 is a psalm of arrival, a song of exultant praise sung in the very presence of the Lord. Pilgrims bless their Lord and receive His blessing.

Jesus and the Psalms

The rationale for these chapters was inspired by Dietrich Bonhoeffer, pastor and director of the Confessing Church, who was martyred in 1945 under the regime of Hitler:

> It is the Son of God made man, who has borne all our human weakness in his own flesh, who here [in the Psalter] pours out the heart of all mankind before God, who stands in our place and prays for us. He has known pain and anguish, guilt and death more deeply than we have. Thus it is the prayer of that humanity he has assumed that comes before God in the Psalms. It is indeed our prayer, but since he knows us better than we know ourselves, since for our sake he became true man, it is also truly his

prayer, and it can only become our prayer because it was his.[3]

The book of Psalms formed the hymn book and prayer book that Jesus would have used when He was growing up and in His adult life. When Joseph and Mary took Jesus to the temple in Jerusalem at the age of twelve, He may well have known by heart the Psalms of Ascents sung along the way by all those travelling with them. This annual journey was long, arduous and sometimes dangerous, but it was also a time of great celebration and joy. We can imagine the families and community groups singing these psalms together as they walked day by day to Jerusalem.

By the time Jesus started His ministry at the age of thirty, He had a thorough knowledge of all the Jewish sacred scriptures, but it is the Psalms that He quoted in His teaching more than any other Old Testament book. We can quite reasonably infer from the tradition and teaching of His upbringing and the discipline and practice of His daily devotions that the Psalms were uppermost and highly formative in His prayers:

I always tell my classes that the book of Psalms formed the hymn book and prayer book that Jesus would have used when he was growing up and in his adult life. I suggest to them that if the gospels tell us what our Lord said and did, then the Psalms

---

[3] Dietrich Bonhoeffer, *The Psalms: Prayer Book of the Bible* (Oxford, SLG Press, 1989), p6.

inform us as to what he thought and felt. They are a
mirror on his inner spiritual life.[4]

Each chapter starts with a study of the psalm in question
followed by a reflection on how Jesus might have read and
prayed it in His last days on earth. We move on from there
to see how we can use each psalm to help us to follow Him
and pray day by day on our own journey. The last section
of each chapter encourages our personal response and
prayer.

Unless stated otherwise, I have used the New Revised
Standard Version (Anglicised) throughout.

---

[4] Quotation from a personal email from Dr Richard S Hess,
Distinguished Professor of Old Testament and Semitic Languages,
Denver Seminary, Colorado, USA. Used with permission.

1
Psalm 120
Far From Home

> [1] *In my distress I cry to the LORD,*
> *that he may answer me:*
> [2] *'Deliver me, O LORD,*
> *from lying lips,*
> *from a deceitful tongue.'*
> [3] *What shall be given to you?*
> *And what more shall be done to you,*
> *you deceitful tongue?*
> [4] *A warrior's sharp arrows,*
> *with glowing coals of the broom tree!*
> [5] *Woe is me, that I am an alien in Meshech,*
> *that I must live among the tents of Kedar.*
> [6] *Too long have I had my dwelling*
> *among those who hate peace.*
> [7] *I am for peace;*
> *but when I speak,*
> *they are for war.*

Introducing Psalm 120

This psalm is a cry from the heart of a pilgrim in great distress. Home seems far away and there is a deep longing to be where safety and truth rule the day rather than experiencing the constant buffeting of conflict and lies. It is an uncomfortable psalm; it might seem a strange song to open this pilgrims' songbook.

The first two verses set the scene. The pilgrim's distress is threatening to destroy trust in the Lord, and there is a wrenching cry from the heart as he realises that he is surrounded by untruthful people who offer advice that is twisted and leads only to trouble. Whispering lips speak words that pierce the pilgrim's heart, causing pain and anguish as faith is questioned and mocked. It almost seems as if the destination on which the heart has been set is far too distant and the journey much too arduous.

It happens so often in the psalms that in naming and addressing a problem before the Lord, faith that was weak and failing is transformed into faith that is strong and persevering, as described in verses 3-4. Now there is a tone of defiance rather than distress. The psalmist poses a question to those who have deceived and mocked him, which he can now answer for himself: 'Do you really think your deceit can rule the day? God, the warrior, has arrows of truth which are far sharper and more potent than the weapons you threaten me with!' Other psalms speak of arrows of cruelty which are countered by God's all-powerful arrows, or of the Lord's intervention from heaven by shooting arrows to rout the enemy to reverse a situation of grave danger.[1]

This exiled pilgrim now realises that the Lord has even more weapons in His armoury. As if the sharp arrows of a warrior were not enough, He lets it be known that He has burning coals of the broom tree to defend His besieged servant.

---

[1] Psalm 64; Psalm 144:6.

An ancient Jewish commentary on this psalm tells a story:

> Two men going through the wilderness sat down under a broom shrub, gathered some fallen twigs of the broom … and ate their victuals. A year later when they came back into the wilderness to the place of the broom shrub and found the ashes of the fire which they had kindled, they said, It is now twelve months since we came through here and ate in this place. Thereupon, they raked up the ashes and as they walked over them, their feet were burnt by the coals under the ashes, for they were still unextinguished.[2]

The coals of fire that the psalmist speaks of were made from the wood of the broom tree and shot on the arrows of warriors in order to set fire to a city under siege. These glowing embers of broom, which burned slow and long, are added to the Lord's arrows fired against the deceit and lies of the pilgrim's adversary. His actions are completely effective against those who were attacking and conspiring against the psalmist.

Living in a country where exiles are unsafe and under attack, far from the place where God dwells, the psalmist repeats in verses 5-7 his distress in a different form. 'It is,' he declares, 'as if I lived among the people of Meshech or Kedar.' The people of Meshech were a barbaric and remote tribe from Turkey; the desert people of Kedar were nomadic Arabian shepherds living between Egypt and

[2] www.matsati.com/wp-content/uploads/2012/10/Midrash-Tehillim-Psalms-120.pdf (accessed 18th May 2020).

southern Judah. Both tribes had reputations for fierce cruelty. 'I feel so far from home both geographically and spiritually; it is as if I were actually living with these two tribes,' declares the pilgrim. But in spite of all this, his final statement is one of triumph! In the hostility he is experiencing, he is able to speak peace. Revenge and bitterness are not part of his armoury; judgement has been left to the Lord (vv3-4). The psalmist lives for peace and speaks words of peace even though he is surrounded by lies and deceit. He knows that as one of the Lord's people among those who do not know Him, he must live a life that portrays the peace and favour which is the Lord's gift to His people.

The psalmist's prayers of distress have been heard. At the outset, he addressed God by His covenant name, Yahweh,[3] crying out to the Lord of faithful, covenant love, always present to help, protect and rescue:

> In the case of the divine covenant ... mutuality disappears: the relationship between the sovereign, transcendent God and those on whom he wills to bestow his promises is totally asymmetrical. It comes about without discussion or negotiation; it is an imposition of grace.[4]

---

[3] The translators of most English versions of the Bible adopt the device of translating the divine name *YHWH* as 'LORD' in capital letters to distinguish it from *Adonai*, another Hebrew word rendered 'Lord', for which lower-case letters are used.

[4] Alec Motyer, *Look to the Rock: An Old Testament Background to Our Understanding of Christ* (Leicester, Inter-Varsity Press, 1996), pp42-43.

The One to whom he prayed was the personal God of unchanging nature, whose promises stood for eternity, and who would always be to His people the covenant and faithful God of steadfast love. A quiet acceptance of his exile and alienation is now possible. Prayer to his Lord brought the assurance of safety and the ability to speak words of peace in a distant and dangerous country.

Jesus and Psalm 120

Shortly before His final Passover, Jesus was summoned to the home of Mary and Martha because His close friend Lazarus was ill. When Jesus eventually arrived at their home in Bethany on the Mount of Olives overlooking Jerusalem, it seemed that He was too late. Lazarus had died and had been buried in a nearby tomb for four days.

Three Greek words in John's narrative describe the intensity of Jesus' feelings as He came face to face with the death of Lazarus, the grief of Mary and Martha and the deafening noise of the professional wailers. Jesus was 'greatly disturbed in spirit' (John 11:33), groaning audibly with indignation as He confronted the devastation of death. He was 'deeply moved' (John 11:33) at the ugly intrusion of death into the perfect and beautiful creation which He had spoken into being. He was surrounded by fearful disciples and a grieving family and community. He entered into all this pain as if it were His own and He 'began to weep' (John 11:35). It was not the same as Mary's loud and unrestrained wailing. The incarnate Creator stood in front of the tomb of Lazarus with the bereaved family and their friends and He shed quiet tears. Far from home, He wept in a country where death reigned.

Few passages in the Gospels describe Jesus' feelings with such depth. The whole situation emphasised the pain and loneliness of His exile from the Father's side, especially as the cross came more closely into view.

> Behind death, he saw him who has the power of death and that sin which constitutes the sting of death. His whole being revolted from that final and deepest humiliation, in which the powers of evil were to inflict on him the precise penalty of human sin.[5]

Knowing all that lay ahead of Him, but with a perfect trust in His Father's purposes to bring Him through death, Jesus approached the tomb where Lazarus had been laid. After praying to His Father, He spoke three words calling Lazarus back from death: 'Lazarus, come out' (John 11:43), and Lazarus walked from the tomb alive!

This was the last sign recounted by John before the events leading up to the trial and crucifixion of Jesus, and it became a hugely divisive issue.[6] Mary, Martha and their friends were overjoyed. No words could express their joy. Many others who were visiting Mary and Martha put their faith in Jesus. Some, however, disappeared quietly back over the Mount of Olives to Jerusalem and told the Pharisees what Jesus had done. A meeting of the Sanhedrin, the supreme Jewish judicial council, was summoned. Their intent for many months had been to arrest Jesus, and they seemed to be getting nowhere. Now

---

[5] Benjamin Warfield, *The Person and Work of Christ* (Philadelphia, PA: The Presbyterian and Reformed Publishing Company, 1950), p129.
[6] John 11:45-57.

they were even more determined. Fearful of an uprising centred on Jesus, the prophet from Nazareth, they resolved that He should be killed.

Hearing of this, Jesus slipped away from Bethany, travelling with His disciples some fifteen miles north to an isolated village called Ephraim in the rocky Judaean hills.[7] Here, for a while, He felt safe. Here He could take stock and pray.

Jesus remained there, in hiding from the crowds and the searching eyes of the Jewish authorities, until the time of the Passover drew near. Perhaps the days were spent teaching and reassuring His disciples, but His thoughts and intentions must have been centred on Jerusalem where He was to suffer and die. He would have sensed the impending conflict of Gethsemane, the mockery of the night trial and the agony of crucifixion. He was only too aware of the hatred and trickery of the authorities who were out to catch Him with the smallest slip of the tongue. Every stranger in the village might have been one of their spies, ready to betray Him and lead Him back to Jerusalem for trial.

Ephraim was a lonely village, hidden away in the Judaean hills, surely the last place Jesus wanted to be. Knowing all that was to happen in Jerusalem, there must have been a longing in His heart to be reunited with His Father from whom He had come and to whom He would return.[8] As the time approached to leave Ephraim for the Passover Festival, the words of this first pilgrim psalm

---

[7] John 11:54. See Leon Morris, *The Gospel According to John* (Grand Rapids, MI: William B Eerdmans Publishing Co., 1971), p569.
[8] John 13:1.

which He would have recited on the journey to Jerusalem every year from the age of twelve might well have become His prayer.

Looking around at all that was happening, Jesus was acutely aware that He did not belong to this world. 'He was in the world, and the world came into being through him; yet the world did not know him' (John 1:10). There was no place for Jesus, no understanding of who He was, no opening of the door to receive Him. The world was a place of hatred where He was constantly hounded by the Jewish authorities who were determined to arrest Him and put Him to death. Betrayal awaited Him by Judas Iscariot, one of His own disciples. Even His close friend Simon Peter would later deny Him. The lonely weeks in Ephraim emphasised even more strongly than ever before that the world was a place of 'distress' for the One who had come to bring peace and reconciliation. Psalm 120 described His situation so accurately. Opposition, lies and confrontation surrounded Him (vv1-2), and He knew only too well the intensity of the battle that lay ahead (vv6-7). He was an exile in a foreign land far from home (v5), tired and homesick in a broken world that He Himself had spoken into being. His exile would end, but only after He had waged war and defeated the forces of sin and death on the cross. Only this way would the Man 'for peace' (v7) bring forgiveness and reconciliation to men and women.

The time in Ephraim drew to a close. Pilgrims were beginning to gather in readiness for their Passover pilgrimage to Jerusalem. Jesus would soon be joining them, descending to Jericho, and then beginning the dangerous, steep ascent to the Mount of Olives towards Jerusalem.

Reading Psalm 120 as a follower of Jesus

We have seen that as we use the psalms to pray, we pray them with Christ. Such prayer rests completely on who He is and on all that He has done and won for us.

The journey from Ephraim took Jesus to the cross, where He endured appalling suffering, carrying the crippling weight of the world's sin and guilt and receiving from His Father the judgement due to us.

Breaking free from the tomb three days later, He declared that sins could be forgiven, death was defeated. His followers, forgiven and at peace with the Father, have been rescued from the power of darkness and established in the kingdom of God's 'beloved Son', Jesus Christ (Colossians 1:13). His disciples still have their residence permits in this world but they have received new passports and identities as citizens of the kingdom of God. Exiles and strangers in this world on a journey to the New Jerusalem, they have no lasting home here. Followers of Jesus are one with Him, unsettled in this world and longing to be at home with Him in His New Creation.

He completely understands our present weaknesses, failures and temptations. He knows every experience of our lives because He has shared in them Himself. He wept when He shared with Mary and Martha in their uncontrolled grief and He was angry at the devastation wrought by death. He wailed over Jerusalem, its refusal to believe in Him and the judgement that would follow. During His hours of prayer in the Garden, He was 'appalled and profoundly troubled',[9] experiencing there 'a

[9] William L Lane, *The Gospel of Mark* (Grand Rapids, MI: William B Eerdmans Publishing Company, 1974), p516.

mental pain, a distress, which hems in from every side ... and leaves no place for defence'.[10]

Psalm 120 challenges us in two areas. First, we learn from the psalmist's honesty in prayer. We can bring to our Lord the utter reality of our lives, the painful struggles and the intensity of our failures. The One who prayed this psalm Himself has become one with us in all our difficulties and troubles. Unlike us, He came through that depth of suffering and pain without sin and has therefore become for all exiled pilgrims the source of eternal salvation. He stands by us and strengthens us as we cry out to Him for mercy and grace when we are weak and suffering.[11]

Faced with the suffering from which none of us is immune, we can go straight to Jesus, seated and praying for us at the right hand of the Father. We can unburden ourselves of the pain of living in exile: the lying lips, deceitful tongues and the hostilities and conflicts that we experience on differing levels. We can cry out to Him about the heartbreaking agony of broken relationships because He has known this. He is present with us when we face the shock of a serious accident or terminal illness or struggle in the darkness of grief. He understands our wordless groans when we find prayer impossible.

Second, the psalmist's closing words challenge us to live in peace, even though we are living in a world of lies and deceit. Our natural reactions of revenge and unforgiveness cannot be part of our lives. The readiness to respond in anger must be transformed by the gift of the

---

[10] Warfield, *The Person and Work of Christ*, p131.
[11] Hebrews 4:15-16.

Holy Spirit, the gift breathed by Jesus on His disciples when they met Him on the evening of the resurrection.

> Jesus came and stood among them and said 'Peace be with you.' ... When he had said this, he breathed on them and said to them, 'Receive the Holy Spirit.' (John 20:19, 22)

Then we can begin to be those who are for peace, even though all we receive back are words of conflict. As the apostle John put it, living in the love of God with faith in Jesus, the Son of God, is the victory that conquers the world.[12]

When difficulties seem unending, we remind ourselves as we pray that, as followers of Jesus Christ, we have a home with Him in the heavenly places; we have a citizenship in heaven.[13] In Hebrews 12:22, the writer encourages his readers not to give up on their journey to Mount Zion, and he 'uses a classic travel agent's strategy: get them to imagine that they are already there',[14] telling them that they have already 'come to Mount Zion'. Even from afar, the journey's destination is secure because they are travelling with Jesus Christ who has already walked this route. There is a security tag firmly attached to every pilgrim walking with Jesus, which is no more and no less than the gift and inner presence of the Holy Spirit of God.[15] That gift, coupled with the assured promises of God and

---

[12] 1 John 5:1-4.

[13] Philippians 3:20.

[14] Thomas G Long, *Hebrews (Interpretation Bible Commentary)* (Louisville, KY: Westminster John Knox Press, 2012), p137.

[15] Ephesians 1:13-14.

the presence of Jesus ascended at the Father's right hand, guarantees our safe arrival at our destination more certainly than anything else. It is safe to set out on the journey and it is safe to travel!

Responding

When things are hard and the going is tough, do you think that your distress can sometimes seem greater than the Lord you trust?

Why is it so easy to forget that we are exiles in this world rather than remembering that our real identity is as citizens of the kingdom of God?

Are there situations around you where you could be a person for peace rather than for conflict?

2
Psalm 121
Dangerous Journey

[1] I lift up my eyes to the hills –
from where will my help come?
[2] My help comes from the LORD,
who made heaven and earth.
[3] He will not let your foot be moved;
he who keeps you will not slumber.
[4] He who keeps Israel
will neither slumber nor sleep.
[5] The LORD is your keeper;
the LORD is your shade at your right hand.
[6] The sun shall not strike you by day,
nor the moon by night.
[7] The LORD will keep you from all evil;
he will keep your life.
[8] The LORD will keep
your going out and your coming in
from this time on and for evermore.

Introducing Psalm 121

Psalm 121 has been a treasured psalm for God's people down through the ages. Here are promises of guardianship, shelter and safe arrival for the journey, even though threats and dangers abound, both seen and unseen.

The psalm can be read as if two pilgrims are conversing on their way up to one of the great Jewish festivals. They have passed through Jericho and have started ascending to Jerusalem, their final destination.

The first pilgrim asks a question (v1) prompted by the nature of the road from Jericho to Jerusalem: 'Where do I find the strength for this dangerous journey through such a threatening landscape?' The road passed through the Judaean desert mountains. Ahead lay eighteen miles (twenty-nine kilometres) with 1,730 feet (530 metres) of ascent. The ground was rough and slippery, paved with flaky limestone. Steep mountains towered over the road, and deep wadis plunged precipitously below the path. It was a notorious route not only for its difficulty but also for the strong possibility of attack by robbers. Jesus' parable of the Good Samaritan makes this clear. Ascending or descending, pilgrims approached this part of the journey with a sense of impending danger and fear.

Hilltops and mountains in the Old Testament were often places where the shrines and idols of false religions were built. Jehoram, King of Judah in the time of Elijah 'made high places in the hill country of Judah, and led the inhabitants of Jerusalem into unfaithfulness, and made Judah go astray' (2 Chronicles 21:11).[1]

This was the route walked by the boy Jesus with His parents when they went up to Jerusalem for the Feast of the Passover. On the return journey, finding Him missing from their group of pilgrims, Joseph and Mary would

---

[1] See also Jeremiah 3:23; 13:27; 17:2; Ezekiel 6:1-3; Hosea 4:13.

have had to retrace their steps up this steep ascent to Jerusalem before they found Jesus in the temple. The next day would have brought yet another day of danger as the little group of three walked down towards Jericho on their own. Jesus had walked this route frequently as a child and as an adult and knew it well.[2]

Acutely aware of all the dangers of the steep road ahead and realising that help would never be found in the hills that surrounded him, the first pilgrim goes on to answer his own question by declaring that his trust will be in the creator, covenant God who made them: 'My help comes from the LORD, who made heaven and earth' (v2). He is the Sovereign Creator, ruling over all that He has made, and over every danger and peril that threatens. He is the One who will give help, who can take effective and decisive action to assist and protect these vulnerable pilgrims.

The conversation between the two pilgrims continues as the second replies. This pilgrim asks no questions, but speaks to the first with a confident aim of reassurance and encouragement (vv3-8). His reply is shot through with two themes interplaying like tunes in the triumphant finale of a grand symphony.

The first theme is the tune of God's covenant relationship with His people. The One who keeps His people, Israel, throughout the ages is the Lord. He never forsakes His covenant, His mercy is steadfast and enduring, and His love is timeless and utterly secure. He loves His people with an unchanging, eternal love, from which they can never be separated.

---

[2] Luke 2:41-51.

The second theme is the tune of guardianship, which recurs six times in verses 3-8. The Hebrew word *shamar* is repeated like an insistent drumbeat: 'he who keeps you', 'he who keeps Israel', 'the LORD is your keeper', 'the LORD will keep you from all evil', 'he will keep your life', 'the LORD will keep your going out and your coming in'. There is such richness in this one repeated word which can mean to watch over, guard, surround and protect. The second pilgrim spares no effort as he emphasises to his companion the security of the Lord's guardianship.

The covenant Lord will keep His people at all times: when the path trips weary legs and when exhaustion threatens to overwhelm. He will prevent His people from falling as they walk and will guard them as they sleep. Never needing sleep Himself, He is constantly and eternally alert to the needs of His loved pilgrims (vv3-4). They will never have to shout louder to make sure their God is listening to them, as Elijah taunted the prophets of Baal![3]

The covenant Lord will guard when shelter is needed. He will shade His pilgrims from the blazing sun and protect them from the extreme cold of a moonlit, desert night (vv5-6). His accompanying presence is 'a shade by day from the heat, and a refuge and a shelter from the storm and rain' (Isaiah 4:6). The Lord's people are safe throughout their journey, from beginning to end and at every stage in between, through every storm, every battering and every temptation from the evil one (vv7-8).

---

[3] 1 Kings 18:27.

The conversation of this whole psalm is a detailed and thorough articulation of the way God has chosen to love and promised to protect and guard His people.

Jesus and Psalm 121

After His time in Ephraim hiding from the Jewish authorities, Jesus and His disciples headed east across the Jordan. Knowing this was His final journey to Jerusalem, He attempted for the last time to make things clear to His disciples:

> Everything that is written about the Son of Man by the prophets will be accomplished. For he will be handed over to the Gentiles; and he will be mocked and insulted and spat upon. After they have flogged him, they will kill him, and on the third day he will rise again.
> (Luke 18:31-33)

But they could not take it in, and their inability to understand what Jesus told them isolated Him from them as He approached Jerusalem.

Some of the events prior to this final part of the journey underlined the sheer loneliness of Jesus. The rich young ruler could not bring himself to follow Jesus; he could only trust vainly in his own possessions and morality. James and John, the sons of Zebedee, put their own desires first and asked Jesus for a seat next to Him in His coming kingdom.[4]

---

[4] Luke 18:18-23; Mark 10:35-40.

Arriving in Jericho, however, Jesus was encouraged by two examples of obedient faith. The tax collector, Zacchaeus, welcomed Jesus into his house; Bartimaeus, healed of his blindness, praised God and followed Jesus.[5]

It was probably the next morning when Jesus started up the steep ascent to Jerusalem. Luke makes the telling comment that Jesus 'went on ahead, going up to Jerusalem' (Luke 19:28), suggesting that the disciples lagged behind Him. Nearly every event since leaving Ephraim had underlined the fact that He was continually misunderstood. No one in the group travelling with Him could begin to understand why He was so determined to go up to Jerusalem, the place of greatest danger. Jesus was acting in lonely but servant-hearted obedience to His heavenly Father as He set out from Jericho to lay down His life 'a ransom for many' (Matthew 20:28). His security was found solely in His wholehearted commitment to the will of His heavenly Father.

Jesus relied closely on the protection of His Father as He climbed the steep and dangerous road. Every step on that perilous climb was overseen. Knowing the long nights of prayer, the betrayal and mocking trials that lay ahead, He placed himself solely under the shelter of His Father's love and divine purposes. His Father's oversight would never falter or slumber, and His love for His Son, the Israel of God, was utterly secure and eternally changeless.

When the time came for Jesus to hang on the Roman cross in the full glare of the midday sun, He knew He would be fulfilling his Father's will, even though it would

---

[5] Luke 19:1–10; Mark 10:46-52.

mean desertion by His Father in the darkness of the final three hours. When the night came and He was to be laid in the tomb, even though the experience of death would be devastatingly bleak, He knew that His Father would never abandon Him in the realm of the dead (vv5-6).[6]

All that was planned by the evil and scheming authorities in Jerusalem could never ultimately harm Him. He would be kept in His dying and in His rising, just as He had been kept in His birth and in the days and years that followed (vv7-8).

Eighteen miles later, after 3,500 feet of ascent up the treacherous road, the group came to the summit of the Mount of Olives and looked across the Kidron Valley towards Jerusalem. Knowing all that lay ahead, Jesus was secure in his Father's purposes and love. He was safe.[7]

He went straight to the house of Mary, Martha and Lazarus in Bethany and spent the night there, receiving their loving hospitality and finding there a place of calm as the storm gathered.

A note on 'Israel' in the Psalms of Ascents

There are nine references to Israel in the fifteen Psalms of Ascents and the first is in Psalm 121. The term applies to all those who have lived and live now by faith in the promises of God which have been fulfilled in Jesus Christ. Jesus is the perfect fulfilment of all the promises and prophecies in the Old Testament about the expected Messiah. The people of God after Christ, as Paul explains in Galatians 4:28 and 6:16, are in direct continuity with the

---

[6] See Psalm 16:10.
[7] John 16:32.

people of God before Christ. They are all the Israel of God. 'Christ is all and in all; and those who follow Him are now … "God's Israel," the real thing.'[8]

> Israel is the people chosen by God and called to respond in faith and obedience. Israel is the people on whom the Lord sets his love … Jesus, a literal descendant of Abraham, himself a Jew, is the Israel who is the object of God's love. He is chosen by God and responds in perfect obedience, fulfilling the law and the prophets (Matthew 5:17) and all righteousness (3:15). Since Jesus is the corporate representative of Israel, God now recognizes as Israel all who respond in faith and obedience to the presence and will of God revealed in Jesus.[9]

So when we read about Israel in these psalms, we are reading about the Lord Jesus and all the people of God who have ever lived, who live now and who will come to live by faith and in obedience to God made known in Christ. When we are told that the Lord watches ceaselessly and tirelessly over Israel, we know it was true for the Father's care of His Son during His earthly life and it has been and is now equally true for every one of His people.

---

[8] Gordon Fee, *Galatians, Pentecostal Commentary* (Blandford Forum: Deo Publishing), p253.
[9] David E Holwerda, *Jesus and Israel: One Covenant or Two* (Grand Rapids, MI: William B Eerdmans Publishing Company, 1995), pp56-57.

Praying Psalm 121 as a follower of Jesus

Climate change, a worldwide pandemic, war in Europe and the cost-of-living crisis have combined to bring a palpable sense of fear about what the future might hold. No wonder that people are asking, 'Where is God in all this? How can there be a loving God if He allows all this to happen?' Just how do we pray when everything seems dark and dangerous, when words fail us and faith falters?

The darkest forces were gathering against Jesus as He climbed the dangerous and precipitous road to Jerusalem. He was acutely aware of this and had warned His disciples, 'We must work the works of him who sent me while it is day; night is coming when no one can work' (John 9:4). He told the crowds surrounding Him in the temple area during passion week to 'Walk while you have the light, so that the darkness may not overtake you' (John 12:35). John's words as Judas left the Upper Room to betray Jesus are so telling: 'After receiving the piece of bread, he immediately went out. And it was night' (John 13:30). How did Jesus pray at this time? He prayed in Gethsemane, after hours of intense struggle, 'Father … not my will but yours be done' (Luke 22:42).

Did things change after Jesus had prayed? It seemed as if the darkness only intensified. Jesus said to those who had come to arrest Him, 'When I was with you day after day in the temple, you did not lay hands on me. But this is your hour, and the power of darkness' (Luke 22:53). The end of it all culminated in the three hours of darkness which came over the whole land as Jesus, separated from His Father, bore our sin and guilt. The Son of God battled with and triumphed over every force of evil in those dark hours and emerged with a cry of desertion that admitted the depth and intensity of all He had suffered. But after everything He had endured, His final prayer was one of assured trust: 'Jesus, crying with a loud voice, said, "Father, into your hands I commend my spirit!" Having said this, he breathed his last' (Luke 23:46).

The prayers of our Lord in Gethsemane and on the cross are examples for every Christian enduring trial and suffering that overwhelms and makes prayer almost impossible. One is a prayer of complete submission to the Father's will; the other is a prayer entrusting all we have and all we are into the Father's hands. Praying thus is exactly the way Jesus taught His disciples to pray:

> Our Father in heaven,
> hallowed be your name.
> Your kingdom come.
> Your will be done,
> on earth as it is in heaven.
> (Matthew 6:9-10)

Though it might seem as if our prayers in such situations achieve little, the truth is that every such prayer of a Christian pilgrim to the Father brings the final establishment of Christ's kingdom one step nearer. If that were not so, would Jesus have told us to pray for the coming of the kingdom, for the will of our Father to be done here on earth as well as in heaven? Answers may seem elusive as we plead with our Father, trying to shut out the voices that cry, 'What sort of God allows this sort of thing to happen?'

But in all our questioning, answers are only found in an implicit trust and confidence in our Father, the Creator of heaven and earth. Yes, we believe that in Christ, through His incarnation, crucifixion, resurrection and ascension, the kingdom of God has been irrevocably established. But in this world, we only know that reign as the Holy Spirit works in us. We live in a world of pain and darkness, but the Spirit nudges us in hope and actuality towards a coming creation, where sin and darkness will be no more as the kingdom of God is fully revealed in Jesus Christ. That is what New Testament theologians call the 'now and not yet' of the Christian life. We wait with longing for all that will be so wonderfully revealed in the new creation that God has in store for His people. Our part is to trust and pray as we have been taught by the Lord Jesus, because every time we ask for His kingdom to come, it edges just one step nearer.

> To pray the second petition of the Lord's Prayer, 'Your kingdom come on earth as it is in heaven' is one of, if not *the* most radical things a human being can do, for it turns out that in this petition we are asking God to bring about the most massive revolution possible.[10]

Obedience to the command of Jesus to pray this petition with every step we take on the steep and dangerous journey, achieves the seemingly impossible task of shifting the tectonic plates of the kingdom of God so that they

---

[10] Darrell W Johnson, *Fifty-Seven Words That Change the World: A Journey Through the Lord's Prayer* (Vancouver: Regent College Publishing, 2005), p42.

encroach just that bit further on the tectonic plates of the kingdoms of this world.

A friend from Central Africa told me about a time when his home town had been overtaken by rebel militia soldiers and flight was the only option for him, his wife, their new baby and their toddler son. Under fire, they fled away from the town, not realising that they were heading straight into an area of fighting and gunfire. Carrying their two children, they vanished into the jungle and hid there as long as they dared, surviving only on mangoes and rice and trying to keep their children quiet as rebel troops passed by. After much prayer, they felt that the time had come for them to attempt the perilous journey to safety. Their final escape was to a nearby airport, lying hidden on the back of a lorry laden with heavy stones. The plane waiting for them could not stop longer than a few minutes because there was a problem with the engine. But they scrambled aboard and arrived safely with friends in a neighbouring country. Looking back on that journey, their testimony is of the Lord's complete protection, even though they feared for their lives. The Lord, in whom they placed their trust, had protected them.

As we ask in the darkest of times where our help comes from, we discover that it does not come from anything that is around us, however seemingly great and powerful. Our help comes only from the Lord, the Creator of heaven and earth, who through Jesus has established 'a kingdom that cannot be shaken' (Hebrews 12:28) and who will finally triumph as the kingdoms of this world become the 'kingdom of our Lord and of his Messiah' who will 'reign for ever and ever' (Revelation 11:15).

The nonconformist minister and hymn writer, Isaac Watts, summed it up:

> Should all the hosts of death,
> And powers of hell unknown,
> Put their most dreadful forms
> Of rage and mischief on,
> I shall be safe, for Christ displays
> Superior power, and guardian grace.[11]

Responding

Looking back on your journey, can you recall times when you realised that the Lord had protected and guided you?

Are there things in your life that make you fearful about the road ahead?

As we cry out to our Lord in situations that test us to the limit, He speaks to us in this psalm and tells us that His covenant of love rests eternally on us so that we can never be separated from Him. It is as if He is saying, 'I watched over my Son, and you are hidden in Him. I will keep you from all harm. I will watch over your life and over your coming and going, now and always.' As you think and pray over this, how might you respond to the Lord?

---

[11] Verse 12 of the original hymn by Isaac Watts (1674–1748), 'Join All the Glorious Names'.

3
Psalm 122
Jerusalem in Sight!

¹*I was glad when they said to me,*
'Let us go to the house of the LORD!'
   ²*Our feet are standing*
within your gates, O Jerusalem.
   ³*Jerusalem – built as a city*
that is bound firmly together.
   ⁴*To it the tribes go up,*
the tribes of the LORD,
as was decreed for Israel,
to give thanks to the name of the LORD.
⁵*For there the thrones for judgement were set up,*
the thrones of the house of David.
   ⁶*Pray for the peace of Jerusalem:*
'May they prosper who love you.
   ⁷*Peace be within your walls,*
and security within your towers.'
   ⁸*For the sake of my relatives and friends*
I will say, 'Peace be within you.'
⁹*For the sake of the house of the LORD our God,*
I will seek your good.

Introducing Psalm 122

A pilgrim's joy (vv1-2)

'In Jerusalem was the temple ... the place of the presence of God on earth. ... To the temple, three times a year, the whole world of Jewry streamed.'[1] Jewish law stated that all were commanded to appear before the Lord in Jerusalem for the three major feasts: Passover, Pentecost and Tabernacles. Psalm 122, with other psalms, demonstrates the great rejoicing and singing that accompanied these pilgrimages which focused on the city of Jerusalem, the Jewish capital. It was here that the Lord had promised to be present with His people in the temple, so setting out for Jerusalem was an occasion of immense excitement, regardless of the hardships of the journey that lay ahead.

Reading the psalm, the joyful anticipation of actually standing within the gates and walls of Jerusalem is tangible. The goal of the pilgrimage has been reached. The months of planning for the journey and the burden of each day's travel are forgotten as Jerusalem comes into sight.

Arriving in Jerusalem (vv3-5)

After all the hazards of the journey recounted in Psalm 121, Jerusalem was a place of refuge and safety, a city built on a rock, surrounded by deep valleys, its houses crowded around narrow streets.

The pilgrims' sense of security on arrival in Jerusalem may well be related to the Jewish tradition of cities of

---

[1] Joachim Jeremias, *Jerusalem in the time of Jesus* (London, SCM Press Ltd, 1969), p75.

refuge. When the Israelites entered the Promised Land, six cities of refuge were established as places of sanctuary for those who had unintentionally killed someone. One of these cities was Hebron, David's capital until he established a new seat of government at Jerusalem. Hebron's status as a city of refuge could well have been transferred to David's new capital. This view is supported by the account of Joab's unsuccessful attempt to find refuge in 'the tent of the LORD' (1 Kings 2:28) during the palace intrigues of Solomon's early reign, and by Isaiah's statement: 'the LORD has founded Zion, and the needy among his people will find refuge in her' (Isaiah 14:32).

As well as a place of security, Jerusalem was a place of gathering, worship and justice. The gathering of thousands of faithful Jewish people and their participation together in the worship that accompanied their great festivals brought enormous joy.[2] They had journeyed to praise their God in His presence in His temple. They had arrived in the city where 'the thrones for judgement' (v5) stood. It was the centre of government and the place where judicial decisions were made which affected the rights and protection of all Jewish people. The strong tradition of justice stemming from the city is expressed in the psalms and reinforced in the Messianic prophecies of the King who is to come.[3]

Praying for Jerusalem (vv6-9)

The pilgrim insists on prayers for Jerusalem and its peace. The word used for 'pray' is an everyday word, rather than

---

[2] See Psalm 48:9-11.
[3] See Psalm 72; Isaiah 32:1.

the formal word used for prayer in a service of worship. 'It is the word Hebrews would use to ask for a second helping of potatoes if still hungry, or for directions if lost.'[4] It is an asking that is repetitive and should be part of the fabric of everyday life.

Pilgrims are to pray for peace, for *shalom*. The word *shalom* (Hebrew for peace) is a word that encompasses the whole of life lived in the shelter of God's covenant love where peace, health, safety and well-being are found. Such peace results in 'a spiritually mature, healthy and integrated personality that serves God and man to the full'.[5] Blessed with this *shalom*, life can be lived in the presence of the Lord, assured of His promises of protection and peace in a world full of danger and conflict.

Jesus and Psalm 122

To understand the relevance of this psalm to Jesus, we must understand the nature of His relationship both to the temple in Jerusalem and to the city of Jerusalem itself.

Jesus had visited Jerusalem from His early childhood, as we have already seen. During His ministry, John records, Jesus went to Jerusalem four times before the week of His crucifixion. These four visits were marked by rising conflict with the religious leaders in the city which moved to a climax during His final week there. The first visit for Passover included a dramatic cleansing of those

---

[4] Eugene H Peterson, *A Long Obedience in the Same Direction: Discipleship in an Instant Society* (Downers Grove, IL: InterVarsity Press, 1980), p52.
[5] R K Harrison, *Numbers: An Exegetical Commentary* (Grand Rapids, IL: Baker Book House, 1992), p133.

selling animals and birds for sacrifices and exchanging money from the temple courts. When He visited the city for an unnamed festival, He came into serious conflict with the religious leaders because He healed a man on the Sabbath. He refused at first on another occasion to go up to Jerusalem for the commencement of the Feast of Tabernacles because He was aware of the murderous intentions of the Jewish leaders. Arriving quietly halfway through the festival, He taught in the temple courts, much to the anger of the authorities who could not even, although they tried, lay a hand on Him. Arriving in Jerusalem at the Feast of Dedication for the last time before His passion, His presence gave rise to even more opposition and an attempt to stone Him.[6]

Why this growing conflict? John gives us the answer when He states categorically in His prologue that 'the Word became flesh and lived among us' (John 1:14). Prior to His coming, the temple was the place where God dwelt, the place where sacrifice was made for sin; but no longer! Now, 'the flesh and blood of Jesus, this man, is the temple where God dwells in the fullness of grace and truth'.[7] Every time Jesus arrived in Jerusalem, the fact that God no longer was present in the Holy of Holies at the heart of the temple building was dramatically emphasised. The true, living temple walked in the temple buildings and spoke with the people of Jerusalem. Here was God made flesh,

[6] See John 2:13-25; 5:1-18; 7:1-32; 10:22-39.
[7] Lesslie Newbigin, *The Light Has Come: An Exposition of the Fourth Gospel* (Grand Rapids, IL: William B Eerdmans Publishing Company, 1982), p33.

God *templing* in human flesh. Conflict was inevitable and unavoidable.

But in spite of all this conflict, the heart of Jesus overflowed with love for the city and people of Jerusalem. He cried out:

> Jerusalem, Jerusalem, the city that kills the prophets and stones those who are sent to it! How often have I desired to gather your children together as a hen gathers her brood under her wings, and you were not willing!
> (Luke 13:34)

We see His deep love for the city again on His eventual arrival in Jerusalem. Journeying from Bethany towards the Kidron Valley, Jesus viewed the whole city spread out before Him. Those surrounding Him would never forget the pained cry that was torn from His heart:

> As he came near and saw the city, he wept over it, saying, 'If you, even you, had only recognized on this day the things that make for peace! But now they are hidden from your eyes. Indeed, the days will come upon you, when your enemies will set up ramparts around you and surround you, and hem you in on every side. They will crush you to the ground, you and your children within you, and they will not leave within you one stone upon another; because you did not recognize the time of your visitation from God.
> (Luke 19:41-44)

This is one of only two recorded occasions when we read of Jesus weeping, but there may well have been other times, as implied by the writer of the epistle to the Hebrews.[8] His tears as He stood weeping over Jerusalem give us a glimpse into the sheer depth and intensity of His love for the city and its people. Prayer for the peace of Jerusalem was at the heart of His mission. With the psalmist, He rejoiced to be there; He loved everything the city represented, but He was cut to the heart by its refusal to recognise Him and the realisation of its ultimate destiny.

Arriving in Jerusalem for the last time, Jesus came into such violent conflict with the authorities that it led to His crucifixion and death. It was the only way that the peace of Jerusalem could be re-established for eternity.

In contrast to the pilgrims of Psalm 122, there was no rejoicing as Jesus came to Jerusalem to face the last week of His life on earth. He wept as He arrived, and He found no refuge there. Gathered with His friends in the Upper Room, there was little sense of unity. They questioned Him, confused about what was happening. Judas walked out into the darkness to betray his Master. Later, nearly all of them fled, and Peter denied any allegiance to Jesus. The last thing that Jesus found in the city was justice as He was dragged before different authorities and courts; it was all a mockery of justice. Why were none of this psalm's pleadings answered for Him?

On His arrival in Jerusalem, Philip told Jesus that there were some Greek pilgrims who wanted to meet Him. Hearing this, Jesus told His disciples that the time had

---

[8] Hebrews 5:7.

come for Him to be glorified. That could only happen if He, like a grain of seed, died and was buried.[9] Only by the death of the Son of Man could salvation come to men and women. Realising fully all that this meant for Him, He cried out to his Father, saying:

> 'Now my soul is troubled. And what should I say –
> "Father, save me from this hour"? No, it is for this
> reason that I have come to this hour. Father, glorify
> your name.' Then a voice came from heaven, 'I have
> glorified it, and I will glorify it again.'
> (John 12:27-28)

Our Lord's sacrifice on the cross and all He achieved there for our salvation was purposed before creation, as Jim Packer explains:

> Scripture is explicit on the fact that from eternity, in
> light of human sin foreseen, a specific agreement
> existed between the Father and the Son that they
> would exalt each other in the following way: the
> Father would honor the Son by sending him to save
> lost sinners through a penal self-sacrifice leading to
> a cosmic reign in which the central activity would
> be the imparting to sinners through the Holy Spirit
> of the redemption he won for them; and the Son
> would honor the Father by becoming the Father's
> love-gift to sinners and by leading them through the

---

[9] John 12:20-24.

Spirit to trust, love and glorify the Father on the model of his own obedience to the Father's will.[10]

Jesus explained to His disciples that He had come to Jerusalem in order to fulfil His Father's will. This would involve His death by crucifixion when He would bear upon Himself the sin, guilt and judgement of humankind. Only that way could sin and evil be vanquished. Only by His rising from death could His followers be with Him in the glory of the New Jerusalem. His sole purpose and aim was to bring glory to His Father, and it was only by following that path that the pleadings of this psalm for peace and justice could be answered.

Reading Psalm 122 as a follower of Jesus

For the follower of Jesus, pilgrimage to Jerusalem is pictured very differently in the New Testament. The incarnation of the Son of God changed everything. The temple, built in the holy city and revered as the place where God dwelt, was now radically relocated in the person of Jesus Christ, God made flesh, in whom 'the whole fullness of deity dwells bodily' (Colossians 2:9).

Our goal as pilgrims now is not the earthly, geographical Jerusalem. It is the New Jerusalem, which is revealed in John's Revelation as appearing from heaven, the place where God will live among His people as their God.[11]

---

[10] J I Packer, *An Introduction to Covenant Theology*, www.kobo.com/gb/en/ebook/an-introduction-to-covenant-theology (accessed 27th March 2023).
[11] Revelation 21:2-3.

John defines his vision further:

> I saw no temple in the city, for its temple is the Lord
> God the Almighty and the Lamb. And the city has
> no need of sun or moon to shine on it, for the glory
> of God is its light, and its lamp is the Lamb. The
> nations will walk by its light, and the kings of the
> earth will bring their glory into it.
> (Revelation 21:22-24)

When we come to the New Testament, the Old Testament
concept of pilgrimage to the earthly city of Jerusalem is
transformed into a life's journey with Christ towards a
New Jerusalem in the new heaven and earth described in
Revelation 21 and detailed graphically in Hebrews 12.

So what does Psalm 122 teach us as followers of the
Lord Jesus about praying? Taking the same headings and
division of the psalm that we used earlier, we can see how
it encourages us to pray as we journey to the heavenly city.

A pilgrim's joy (vv1-2)

The joy of all those who set their minds and hearts on the
hope that is in Christ is a far greater joy than that shared
by pilgrims as they set out for the Passover feast in
Jerusalem. Our joy is not set on an earthly city which is
temporal, but on a heavenly and eternal city. Our joy is
indescribable and filled with glory, says Peter, as we set
our hope on all that will be ours 'when Jesus Christ is
revealed' (1 Peter 1:3-9).

But sometimes the difficulties of the journey weigh us
down and we lose sight of the heavenly city. It can seem
as if we are stumbling through a deep valley with our

destination out of sight. However, we are constantly reminded that we have One with us who has promised to accompany us with His personal presence every step of the way: 'Remember,' said Jesus, 'I am with you always, even to the end of the world' (Matthew 28:20, J B Phillips).

Every step taken towards our destination when difficulties and suffering rule the day, even though it may not seem so, is to be a step forward in our growth in Christ, another opportunity to allow the love of God to be poured extravagantly into our hearts by the Holy Spirit. We must trust that this strength and joy imparted by the Holy Spirit will be sufficient for our praying on the journey.

Arriving in Jerusalem (vv3-5)

The writer of the epistle to the Hebrews encourages us to run the race 'set before us' with our eyes fixed on Jesus (Hebrews 12:1-2). But only a few verses later, he tells us that we have already arrived at our destination.

When we arrive at the new Mount Zion, there is no shrinking back or trembling, no dark cloud or thunder and no trumpets to warn us against stepping onto holy ground. There is no voice that thunders, causing us to fear. The blessing on our arrival is one of unqualified and joyful welcome, exuberant celebration and glorious reunions with all those who have been brought finally to this indefinably safe and assured place through Christ.[12] The psalmist's prayer of verse 5a has been answered.

This is the glorious tension of New Testament theology. Jesus, through His sacrifice on the cross, has promised to bring us to this heavenly city. But this is not merely a

---

[12] See Hebrews 12:18-24.

future promise; all its blessings are experienced and known as true in the here and now for every Christian, as we saw when we looked at Psalm 121. As we journey, constantly tempted by sin, we also live as those who have been raised with Christ and seated with Him in 'heavenly places', as Paul explains in Ephesians 2:6. Mount Zion, the new Jerusalem, where God will dwell among us, is our goal. But even now, God lives with us, His life in our life as the Holy Spirit makes His home in us. Every day on the journey is another day with the Lord Jesus. We are encouraged because we know that on arrival at our destination, we will see Him and know Him in a fuller way than we could ever imagine. Our destination, as stated in Hebrews 12:18-24, is the place where angels celebrate eternally, the place where we will join them, rejoicing alongside all our brothers and sisters in Christ. It is a place of righteous judgement and a place of unimaginable safety, secured by an eternal covenant sealed with the shed blood of the Son of God on a Roman cross.

Now we have fuel for effective prayer. Now we can 'lift … drooping hands and strengthen … weak knees' (Hebrews 12:12). The race demands perseverance, but as we run we also reckon that we have already arrived at our destination. 'Our feet are standing within your gates, O Jerusalem!' (v2). Scripture teaches and experience proves that our faith is refined in the hardest times. Suffering and severe testing are to be endured simultaneously with the certain knowledge that our lives are safe, 'hidden with Christ in God' (Colossians 3:3).

Praying for the peace of Jerusalem (vv6-9)

The Hebrew for peace (*shalom*), which occurs three times in the last four verses of this psalm, is used throughout the Old Testament as a greeting and as a blessing. The priestly benediction in Numbers 6:24-26 bestows the blessing of peace upon God's people. That blessing finds its fulfilment in Jesus, the risen Prince of Peace. Meeting His disciples on the evening of the first Easter Day, He said to them, 'Peace be with you' (John 20:19, 21). Many of the New Testament epistles contain a greeting very similar to the one with which Paul starts his letter to the church in Rome: 'Grace to you and peace from God our Father and the Lord Jesus Christ' (Romans 1:7).

The meanings of the word 'peace' in the Old and New Testaments are identical, a prayer that every detail of our lives may be lived under the protection of God's covenant love. There we are promised a safe journey, an assured arrival and a secure eternity.

The promise of the Lord Jesus is to guide our feet into the way of peace.[13] Our aim and prayer, along with all those who journey with us, must be to walk in peace with our brothers and sisters in Christ. To think of arriving at the heavenly city alongside fellow pilgrims with whom we are not on speaking terms is a travesty and a denial of every prayer we utter for peace. Sadly, the band of pilgrims *en route* to the New Jerusalem, the city of peace, is far too often and too easily torn apart by futile and unnecessary divisions. We need to pray this psalm far more often!

---

[13] Luke 1:79 (See also 2:14; 19:42).

55

Responding

What might encourage you to share in the real joy of these pilgrims as you prepare to worship the Lord week by week?

Our Christian faith is certainly for the here and now, but even more for all that is to come. Do the problems of today shut out the realities of all that is to come, stored up for us in Christ?

'It is late in the day, and … we are winded and tired.'[14] How do you react (and pray) when your Christian pilgrimage just seems too much to bear and there's a real temptation to throw in the towel?

---

[14] Long, *Hebrews*, p128.

4
Psalm 123
Walking in Dark Valleys

¹ To you I lift up my eyes,
O you who are enthroned in the heavens!
² As the eyes of servants
look to the hand of their master,
as the eyes of a maid
to the hand of her mistress,
so our eyes look to the LORD our God,
until he has mercy upon us.
³ Have mercy upon us, O LORD, have mercy upon us,
for we have had more than enough of contempt.
⁴ Our soul has had more than its fill
of the scorn of those who are at ease,
of the contempt of the proud.

Introducing Psalm 123

This is the first of the Psalms of Ascents to deal specifically with suffering. Here that suffering results from the ridicule and contempt experienced by the psalmist and his friends. The psalm is a cry from the hearts of loyal servants to a trusted Master, a lament from a dark valley by those who are aware that their breaking point is very close. But the servant who leads the prayer is one who knows that the path walked is 'beneath an open heaven. What matter then whether our path runs through dark valleys and awful chasms? We know who is watching over us.'[1] The pilgrim's Master is ruling in heaven. He is not distant but immediately present. He sees and is constantly aware of all that is happening to His servants on earth. He is always present to intervene and protect.

The places where prayer starts (vv1-2)

Prayer starts in the courts of heaven

Bowed down with pain, there is no other place to go. Eyes that were cast downwards are now turned heavenwards, because the only assured and safe source of help is from the One enthroned in heaven. By the time we reach the end of verse 2, the whole group of pilgrims has joined together in crying out for mercy from their Lord.

In the most constrained of circumstances, where bitterness, anger and questions could well have ruled the day, these pilgrims go straight to the One who rules in heaven and holds everything in His hands. Their cry for mercy echoes the desperate prayer of King Hezekiah when Jerusalem was surrounded by the cruel Assyrian army:

> O LORD the God of Israel, who are enthroned above the cherubim, you are God, you alone, of all the kingdoms of the earth; you have made heaven and earth. Incline your ear, O LORD, and hear; open your eyes, O LORD, and see; hear the words of

---

[1] Helmut Thielicke, *Life Can Begin Again: Sermons on the Sermon on the Mount* (London: James Clarke & Co Ltd, 1966), p22.

Sennacherib, which he has sent to mock the living God.
(2 Kings 19:15-16)

Hezekiah's prayer and the prayer of the pilgrims in Psalm 123 start on common ground. First they go straight to the throne of the Ruler of heaven and earth, acknowledging the universal supremacy and rule of the God of Israel, the Lord. Seeing the Lord enthroned in majesty, they state their particular needs and plead for mercy and grace. Both Hezekiah and the pilgrims are pleading in the highest court for deliverance from a foe who has ridiculed them and mocked their God.

Prayer starts in the hearts of the Lord's servants

The cry to the highest throne in the courts of heaven is made from the humblest place: the heart of a manservant or maidservant. Jewish recollections of their own time of slavery in Egypt meant that they regarded those who would have normally been called slaves as people with considerable rights. They were servants, people in the households of the Children of Israel who became part of the communities in which they served and who therefore shared in the covenant privileges of the Lord's people.[2] That is why these pleading servants can use the personal name of God: Yahweh. He has committed Himself to them and they in turn commit themselves to Him in their distress. Their Master is their friend and He is fully aware of their situation and rights.

---

[2] See Deuteronomy 16:9-12.

Experiencing life at its worst, overwhelmed with ridicule and abuse, their prayer comes from utter brokenness and from the lowest ebb. This cry could have ended with an insistence that the Lord should deliver them then and there, but these servants trust their Lord implicitly in spite of everything. Casting themselves on the Lord's mercy, they are prepared to wait patiently until He intervenes to deliver them.

The assurance of God's mercy (vv3-4)

The pilgrims had endured contempt and scorn

The word 'contempt' implies undeserved scorn and shame that strikes at the depths of the heart. It also means to tread down or despise. Those held in contempt are the objects of mockery; they are bullied and shunned. It could have been because they were of small stature or they came from a small family. It might have happened because they were financially poor or infertility had stolen the opportunity of bearing children.[3] To be treated with contempt was to be scorned and shamed, the ultimate disgrace in the East, both then and now. People still, as they did in Old Testament times, seek the honour and affirmation of their fellow-citizens. Dishonour is something to be avoided at all cost, all too easily provoked by non-adherence to common cultural values and traditions. As Derek Kidner puts it in his commentary on

---

[3] My thanks to Dr Emil Shehadah for his help in understanding this concept.

the Psalms, 'other things can bruise, but this is cold steel'.[4] The psalmist is expressing, in the strongest possible terms, feelings of isolation, shame and ridicule.

The pilgrims had endured 'more than enough'

The phrase 'more than enough' literally means 'we are exceedingly full of contempt'.[5] The repetition makes it clear that they are at breaking point in both body and soul. These pilgrims have experienced repeated derision and scorn, and the burden of it has increased until they can bear no more and they cry out in desperation from the depths. What has happened has cut to the very heart of who they are and all that they stand for, and brought them to the limit of what can be borne. 'Enough is enough!' they cry. 'We can bear no more.'

The fact that their wounds have been inflicted by the arrogant and proud has only rubbed more salt into the wounds. With wounds that smart, unable to take any more, beaten to the ground and seemingly defeated, all that is possible now is this cry of brokenness.

The pilgrims' cry for mercy

They cry out from the depths of shame for mercy, knowing that their Lord is enthroned in the heavens. They know that the covenant God of promise can and will in His time restore those who are shamed and humiliated; He is able to remove the cloak of disgrace with His

---

[4] Derek Kidner, *Psalms 73-150: A Commentary on Books III, IV and V of the Psalms (Tyndale Old Testament Commentaries)* (London: Inter-Varsity Press, 1975), p435.

[5] Allen P Ross, *A Commentary on the Psalms, Volume 3 (90–150)* (Grand Rapids, IL: Kregel Academic), p639.

graciousness. Yes, the word for 'mercy' here carries the meaning of *graciousness* as well. In effect, the pilgrims are praying, 'We have been despised and treated ungraciously. Reigning Lord, we kneel before You as Your servants knowing that You can restore our honour and that, in accordance with Your character and name, You will be merciful and gracious.'

The cry for mercy and grace is made twice, the repetition only serving to emphasise the depth of mockery and ridicule that had been experienced.

Jesus and Psalm 123

There is a striking allusion to the start of Psalm 123 in John 17:1, the account of Jesus' High Priestly prayer: 'Jesus … lifted up his eyes to heaven' (John 17:1, KJV).

Approaching the depths of the shame of the cross, Jesus did the same as the servants in this psalm. He prayed for help from His Father, the One enthroned in heaven. The One who was God incarnate became a servant, fulfilling the ministry of the Servant portrayed by Isaiah.[6] He taught about servanthood, telling His followers that they were to be servant-like in their lifestyle and leadership. He lived as a servant, seen most notably as He washed His disciples' feet. He died as a servant, giving His life as a ransom.

Throughout the three years of His earthly ministry, Jesus suffered contempt and ridicule which increased in intensity as Good Friday approached. It came from the authorities and it came from His disciples as they betrayed Him, denied Him and deserted Him. Everything

---

[6] See Matthew 8:17; 12:17-21; Luke 2:32; 22:37; John 12:38.

culminated in the shame of the cross, a death that was among the most feared of all the ways to die because of its utter disgrace and dishonour.

It was on the Roman cross that Jesus totally fulfilled the role of Isaiah's Servant. Suffering in our place, bearing all the sin of the world, its guilt and judgement, He stood as the mediator between us and God. The path He obediently followed was in complete fulfilment of the prophecies about the Suffering Servant. Hanging on the cross, the deep shame of crucifixion was intensified by the mocking words of some of the bystanders:

> Those who passed by derided him, shaking their heads and saying, 'You who would destroy the temple and build it in three days, save yourself! If you are the Son of God, come down from the cross.' In the same way the chief priests also, along with the scribes and elders, were mocking him, saying, 'He saved others; he cannot save himself. He is the King of Israel; let him come down from the cross now, and we will believe in him. He trusts in God; let God deliver him now, if he wants to; for he said, "I am God's Son."' The bandits who were crucified with him also taunted him in the same way.
> (Matthew 27:39-44)

As contempt was piled on contempt and ridicule on ridicule, Jesus reversed the prayer of Psalm 123. The pilgrims pleaded for the grace and mercy of God. The suffering Servant imparted grace and mercy, even though the contempt to which He was subjected was greater than that experienced by any other person. Instead of crying out for mercy for Himself, He prayed for mercy for those who crucified Him and those who mocked Him, saying, 'Father, forgive them; for they do know not what they are doing' (Luke 23:34). He assured the dying thief of His gracious acceptance with the words, 'Truly I tell you, today you will be with me in Paradise' (Luke 23:43). Mercy and grace were extravagantly poured out, as shame and ridicule were extravagantly heaped on the suffering and dying Lord of Glory. The prayer of every shamed pilgrim was answered fully at the cross.

Reading Psalm 123 as a follower of Jesus

Sometimes we feel that things can hardly get any worse. Everything seems to have conspired against us. There may be utter shame for our sin and unbelief or there might be ridicule from those who mock us ruthlessly for our faith, refusing to consider why we might even begin to think of living under the Lordship of Jesus Christ rather than living just for ourselves.

Some suffer abuse and violence in the home, aggravated by their allegiance to Jesus Christ. Others face discrimination and the disgrace of being overlooked for promotion because they are openly Christian in their workplaces, standing against illegal, dishonest or unethical practices. There are countless Christians worldwide who face false accusations, unjust trials and sentences, appalling torture and long, lonely spells of imprisonment. Some even face the threat of death or death itself because they confess Jesus Christ as Lord. Whenever and however suffering and dishonour like this arrive, strength can be sapped and faith can flounder as we wonder how much more we can bear.

That is where this psalm has complete relevance. At our lowest ebb, all we can do (and it is the best we can do) is fall to the ground and lift up our eyes to the Lord enthroned in heaven. It may well be that there are no words to express the depth of our feelings at this point. A sense of guilt can overwhelm us or we may struggle as contempt is heaped on us. We are left senseless, finding trust almost beyond our grasp. The prayer of the psalmist becomes our own prayer as we cry out in despair, trusting with the little faith we can muster that the Master we serve will not only hear us but will also act in grace and mercy towards us.

Shortly after George Matheson[7] had started to study theology at Glasgow University, he was told that he was going blind; there was nothing anyone could do for him. He summoned the courage to tell his fiancée, but she deserted him, realising that marriage would mean a lifetime of care for a blind husband. He became completely reliant on the support of his sister. However, on the evening of her wedding years later, George realised that he would now be without the one person who had cared for him. Facing his blindness without her was intolerable and he became deeply depressed. It was then that he wrote the hymn 'O Love That Wilt Not Let Me Go'. In the last verse, he writes of lying in the dust, his life dead. The only comfort was the cross of Christ:

> O Cross, that liftest up my head,
> I dare not ask to fly from Thee;

---

[7] George Matheson, FRSE (1842–1906) was a Scottish minister, hymn writer and author.

I lay in dust life's glory dead,
And from the ground there blossoms red
Life that shall endless be.

Will the Master hear His servants as they cry out to Him? The answer is a resounding, 'Yes!' There is One who hears the cry of our hearts and takes that cry to the Father. Jesus Christ has walked this path before us and knows everything we experience. He took the burden of our guilt and shame on the cross as He received in His perfect life all the heaped-up sin of humanity and its judgement. The deep shame and contempt of His suffering was transformed into the glory of His resurrection life and His exaltation as King of kings and Lord of lords.[8] Identified with Him in His death, resurrection and exaltation, we live in the wonder of our forgiveness and acceptance with His Father.

Knowing that Jesus has trodden this path, that He walks with us and that the time will come when we shall see Jesus 'as he is' (1 John 3:2), we take heart. Then there will no more need for that cry for mercy. Every wound or hurt will be healed when we meet Him face to face and see for ourselves the scars in His risen body, deeper scars than we could ever carry. This transforming hope, as well as the daily needed grace of forgiveness and strength, is promised to us in Christ with unfathomable assurance.

We must take note, as well, that this psalm is a prayer prayed together by a group of pilgrims who found strength in the fellowship of journeying together. When we have had more than enough of the ridicule and

---

[8] See Revelation 17:14.

suffering of this world, we are not to bear it alone. The Lord Jesus accompanies us by His Holy Spirit, who is a source of great strength. We also travel with those who are our fellow citizens and members together of the Father's family, and we know that we are committed to walk with them through dark valleys and over mountaintops, sharing our sadness and our joy.

When we cry for mercy to our Father in heaven, lifting up our eyes and pleading that He will act in grace and mercy, we know that 'we walk beneath an open heaven. What matter then whether our path runs through dark valleys and awful chasms? We know who is watching over us.'[9]

Responding

Although we believe that God is good, it doesn't stop us from crying out in anger and frustration to Him when everything seems to go wrong. Psalm 73 is a good psalm to pray when we feel like this.

The danger is that when we are in the depths of trouble and difficulty, the last thing we do is pray. When things look so bleak, why do you think we react like this?

Another danger is that we isolate ourselves. This psalmist started to pray alone, but soon joined with others to pray. Is there a lesson for us to learn here?

---

[9] Thielicke, *Life Can Begin Again*, p22.

5
Psalm 124
Godly Remembrance

¹*If it had not been the LORD who was on our side*
– let Israel now say –
²*if it had not been the LORD who was on our side,*
when our enemies attacked us,
³*then they would have swallowed us up alive,*
when their anger was kindled against us;
⁴*then the flood would have swept us away,*
the torrent would have gone over us;
⁵*then over us would have gone*
the raging waters.
⁶*Blessed be the LORD,*
who has not given us
as prey to their teeth.
⁷*We have escaped like a bird*
from the snare of the fowlers;
the snare is broken,
and we have escaped.
⁸*Our help is in the name of the LORD,*
who made heaven and earth.

Introducing Psalm 124

The second of the Psalms of Ascents which deals with suffering uses a way of praying laid down in the psalms. I call this method 'godly remembrance', and one of the best examples of it is in Psalm 77. Asaph, the long-serving leader of music in the reigns of David and Solomon, was overwhelmed by events and cried out to the Lord for help. He was so troubled that sleep was impossible and he felt as if God had deserted him. Eventually he found a way out of this despair:

> I will call to mind the deeds of the Lord;
> I will remember your wonders of old.
> I will meditate on all your work,
> and muse on your mighty deeds.
> (Psalm 77:11-12)

Asaph found his faith restored as he remembered all that God had done for him and his people in the past. He employed the method of 'godly remembrance'. As we come to look at Psalm 124, we find David in a similar situation. The Philistine armies had invaded and defeat seemed inevitable. It was only as he looked back to all that the Lord had done for him and his people in the past that his faith in the Lord was restored.

The Philistines were an ancient people who had settled on the coastal plains of Palestine at about the same time as the Children of Israel arrived in the Promised Land. They troubled the Israelites for years, and having the monopoly on mining and working iron, they had superior weapons and military dominance. At the time, David was establishing his new capital, Jerusalem, and securing its defences.[1] The last thing he needed was a Philistine attack. The Old Testament historians actually record two occasions when the Philistines marched on Jerusalem and made camp in the Valley of Rephaim, a valley that runs south-west from Jerusalem towards the coastal plains.[2] Their encampment was probably just to the south-west of David's new capital, Jerusalem, and the enemy's proximity would have brought fear into the heart of every resident.

We are given the impression (124:1-2) that the inhabitants of Jerusalem had suffered sporadic Philistine raids. Those attacks and the noise they could hear at night from the enemy camp left them feeling as if they were about to be engulfed and swallowed alive. There seemed no way they could survive a full-scale attack. The people's fear is graphically described: they were in danger of being swept away in a torrent of raging water or trapped like a small bird in a hunter's snare. Facing humiliation by the Philistines, David's trust in the Lord was restored by 'godly remembrance'.

David remembered his people's story (vv1-5)

What if the Lord had not been there for us? It's a repeated question (vv1-2) that starts David on a process of remembering. His mind goes back to the story of the Children of Israel's struggle to survive under Pharaoh's mercilessly cruel regime in Egypt. After experiencing the Lord's protection from nine dreadful plagues that afflicted the Egyptians, they had been delivered from the death of

---

[1] Read the story in 2 Samuel 5:4-10.
[2] 2 Samuel 5:17-25; 1 Chronicles 14:8-16.

the firstborn during the final plague by taking the blood of a slain lamb and daubing it on the doorposts of their houses. The Lord told them that He would pass over them when He saw the blood on the doorposts and their firstborns would be safe. Moses instructed them to eat the roasted lamb, have their coat and shoes on and a staff in their hands ready to flee from Egypt. It was the pivotal point of the history of the Children of Israel, a never-to-be-forgotten night. But as they fled, they found themselves trapped between the pursuing armies of Pharaoh and the Red Sea. In obedience to God's specific command, Moses stretched out his hand over the sea and the Lord brought complete deliverance to His people.

Miraculously led on dry land through the parted waters, they turned and watched as the Egyptian armies were engulfed in the raging torrent of the returning sea.[3] The Lord had protected His people, and His salvation became the central point of their annual Passover festival. Safe on the eastern side of the Red Sea, the people sang a triumphant confession of faith and trust, praising their Lord and rejoicing in His strength and protection in the very worst of situations.[4]

The threat of being swallowed up and swept away in the raging sea was abated (vv3-5). What if the Lord had not been there for us then? Facing extreme danger, David remembered the Lord's faithfulness to His people in years past. He wrote this psalm to remind himself of that hymn of praise sung on the eastern shore of the Red Sea. David's

---

[3] Exodus 12, 14–15.
[4] Exodus 15:1-12.

'godly remembrance' restored his trust in his Lord's protection and oversight.

David remembered his own story (vv6-7)

The images in the next two verses are gathered from David's years as a shepherd and the days he spent in the cave of Adullam hiding from King Saul.

Persuading King Saul to let him attack Goliath, the young teenager David told him that when he was keeping his father's sheep and a lion or a bear came and carried off a sheep from the flock, he would go after it, strike it and rescue the sheep. If it turned on him, he would seize it by its hair and kill it. He told King Saul, 'The LORD, who saved me from the paw of the lion and from the paw of the bear, will save me from the hand of this Philistine' (1 Samuel 17:37).

Later, when he was hiding from King Saul in the cave of Adullam in the Judaean hills,[5] David penned Psalms 57 and 142. Psalms 140 and 141 also seem to fit into David's story here. Psalm 57 refers to attack from lions, and all these psalms repeatedly mention the snares described in Psalm 124:6-7. In those treacherous days of flight from Saul, David was led and protected at every twist and turn of the way by the Lord. Now, as king over his people and facing immense danger, he looked back on those days of flight from King Saul and remembered the Lord's protection and guidance.

---

[5] See 1 Samuel 22:1-5.

Godly remembrance leads David to trust (v8)

'What if ...?' asked David. What if the Lord had not been there for His people at the Red Sea? What if the Lord had not intervened for him in the past? As he drew his psalm to a conclusion, David confessed triumphantly that the Philistine threats of danger were no match for the One who watched over him. He would attack the Philistines with victory assured. The Lord dramatically guided David and his army and led them to defeat the Philistine invaders twice. So he ended his psalm with a triumphant confession of praise and trust: 'Our help is in the name of the LORD, who made heaven and earth' (v8).

David had remembered his Lord's deliverance in the past, and his fears and doubts were transformed into a strong, confident trust in the character and actions of his faithful Lord, who 'initiates all things ... maintains them in existence ... controls them in operation ... and directs them to their appointed end'.[6]

Jesus and Psalm 124

All the earthly and military victories of David, King of Israel, were only shadows of the universal and eternal victories of the Lord Jesus. The Gospel writers go to great lengths to remind us repeatedly that Jesus was a direct descendant of King David. When the risen Christ speaks to His church in Philadelphia, one of the seven churches of Revelation, He says that His words are the words of the One who holds the 'key of David' (Revelation 3:7). He

---

[6] Alec Motyer, *Journey: Psalms for Pilgrim People* (Nottingham, Inter-Varsity Press, 2009), p62.

alone has the highest power and authority. He is the new King David and He alone opens and shuts the door to the New Jerusalem, the heavenly city of David. There is no one else with this power to save and this kingly authority.

King David penned Psalm 124 after experiencing imminent attacks from his greatest foes, the Philistines. The incarnate Son of God, 'great David's greater Son',[7] might well have prayed this psalm as He lived in our broken world, experiencing unbelief and hostility from those around Him and constant attack from Satan, His greatest foe.

The nature of those attacks only highlighted the contrast between the pre-incarnate and incarnate experience of Jesus, a contrast far beyond any human understanding. Born as a man, He took upon Himself a ministry of suffering to restore sinful men and women to His Father. Prior to His incarnation, He had enjoyed the serene and unbroken presence of His Father. Nights of prayer in the hills and finally in Gethsemane would have reminded Him of the bliss of the life and glory He had with His Father before the world began. We cannot begin to fathom the comfort this remembrance brought to Him as He endured the continual confrontation with the pain of unbelief, the destructive power of death and the antagonism of the powers of evil, all bringing their untold agony and grief.

The beginning of the public ministry of Jesus was marked by His baptism in the River Jordan. Standing among those whom John was baptising for the repentance

---

[7] This title of Jesus comes from the hymn 'Hail to the Lord's Anointed' by James Montgomery (1771–1854).

of sin, Jesus offered Himself for baptism as the sign of His total identification with sinners and in order 'to fulfil all righteousness' (Matthew 3:15). The Father spoke publicly, saying, 'You are my Son, the Beloved; with you I am well pleased' (Luke 3:22). These words, spoken again at His transfiguration (Matthew 17:5), reinforced memories of His deep and perfect joy in the fellowship of the Trinity. They were words that affirmed and reminded the Son of God throughout His ministry of the glory that He had shared with the Father 'before the world existed' (John 17:5).

Godly remembrance in the wilderness temptations (Luke 4:1-13; Mark 1:12-13)

Immediately after His baptism by John, Jesus was driven out[8] by the Spirit into the Judaean wilderness. Scorched by the sun by day and chilled to the bone in the bitter cold of the desert night, Jesus endured forty days of fasting. Suffering extreme weakness, Jesus was assaulted by the devil, tempting Him to act in a way that denied the central fact of who He was and all He had come to achieve.

He resisted these attacks by remembering the words of Moses to the Lord's people, the Children of Israel, in their desert journey. One commentator gives Deuteronomy 6 the title 'The Threat of Amnesia'.[9] Moses instructed the people when they came into the land that the Lord God was giving them, 'Take care that you do not forget the

---

[8] The Greek word used by Mark is very strong. It has the literal meaning 'thrown out'.

[9] Walter Brueggemann, *Deuteronomy* (Nashville, TN: Abingdon Press, 2001), p81.

LORD, who brought you out of the land of Egypt'
(Deuteronomy 6:12).

They were never to forget that they had been given
bread, meat and water throughout their journey; they
were not to put the Lord to the test as they had done
previously and they were to remember that there was
more to life than the satisfying of their physical needs. All
the words of the Lord their God were to provide their vital
and constant nourishment and strength. Remembering the
Lord's protection of His ancient people, His presence with
them in their desert wanderings and His words of promise
given through Moses, Jesus found strength to endure and
resist the devil.

As well as remembering the story of the Children of
Israel, Jesus would have remembered and relied totally on
the words of His Father at His baptism, assuring Him of
His Father's love and pleasure.

Godly remembrance in His ministry (Matthew 11:25-30)

John the Baptist, imprisoned by Herod, sent messengers to
Jesus to ask if He was 'the one who is to come' (Matthew
11:3). Jesus told them to tell John that he was to look at the
evidence which bore witness to the fact that He was the
Messiah and that He was doing precisely all that had been
foretold about the Messiah by the prophets. Jesus went on
to say that those who were not offended by this evidence
of His miracles and preaching were blessed, but that there
were many who were deaf to His words and blind to His
miracles. They would be judged for this refusal to repent
and believe. Such stubborn unbelief and its dreadful
consequences hurt Jesus deeply and He took refuge in His
relationship with His Father.

All things have been handed over to me by my Father, and no one knows the Son except the Father, and no one knows the Father except the Son and anyone to whom the Son chooses to reveal him. (Matthew 11:27)

As He remembered His place from eternity with His Father, Jesus continued on His journey to Jerusalem and the cross. He had found strength and comfort in godly remembrance.

The prayer of Jesus as He faces the cross

Jesus was facing the unimaginable agony of the cross, its cruel and intense physical pain, and the utter darkness of being separated from His Father as He suffered for sin and bore the judgement of the world. His hour had come and we are allowed to hear His prayer: 'I glorified you on earth by finishing the work that you gave me to do. So now, Father, glorify me in your own presence with the glory that I had in your presence before the world existed' (John 17:4-5).

Facing the cross, He remembered the glory He had shared with His Father before the creation of the world, and He prayed that He would be glorified in His Father's presence on His triumphant return to the courts of heaven.

Having completed all the work, having done everything which the Father had appointed him to do, he asks, as it were: Has not the time now arrived when I can come back to you, exactly where I was before? I have done the work. 'Father, glorify thou me with thine own self with the glory which I had with thee before the world was.' But the astonishing

77

thing for us to remember at this point is that he goes back as God-Man! In eternity he was God the Son, pure deity, and he shared the glory, but now he goes back as God-Man. And as God-Man, and our representative, the glory which he momentarily laid aside at the request of the Father is restored to him, and thus as God-Man and Mediator he again shares this ineffable glory of the eternal God.[10]

Reading Psalm 124 as a follower of Jesus

We all face situations at times that test us to the limit. Like King David, circumstances can take hold of us and sweep us along as if we are caught in a raging torrent, or they can leave us feeling trapped like a snared bird. When that happens, it is so easy to lose sight of the Lord. Sleep becomes difficult and our spirits sink.

This psalm reminds us that there is a way out of these circumstances. The rediscovery of the presence of our Lord and renewed trust are encouraged if we can ask the question, 'What if the Lord had not been there for us?'

The most important 'godly remembrance' for any Christian pilgrim is in obedience to the command of Jesus in the Upper Room: 'Do this in remembrance of me' (Luke 22:19). As we take bread and wine at the Lord's Supper in memory of His broken body and shed blood, we realise the fact that Christ is united with us and we are united with Him on our journey. This remembering, which Paul states is actually proclamation,[11] is to be repeated again

---

[10] D Martyn Lloyd-Jones, *Saved in Eternity: God's Plan of Salvation* (Eastbourne: Kingsway Publications, 1990), p77.
[11] 1 Corinthians 11:26.

and again until the Lord Jesus returns. Remembrance will then be gloriously replaced with reality.

I said at the beginning of this chapter that Psalm 77 was one of the best examples of 'godly remembrance'. Starting my theological studies, I came face to face for the first time with conflicting views about the Christian faith and the validity of Scripture. It was a difficult time. Certainties I had lived with till then were thrown into the melting pot and my faith was severely tested. What was true and what was false? Wandering in that wilderness, I came across Psalm 77 and read of Asaph's determination in verses 11-12 (quoted at the start of this chapter) to call to mind the deeds of the Lord, His miracles, His works and His deeds. It was like a wake-up call for me. I set out on the path of 'godly remembrance' and gradually faith was restored.

I have used 'godly remembrance' many times since! It brings comfort, strength, peace, hope and light to the path we tread. We will be able to say that if the Lord had not been on our side, then we would have been overcome by the dangers we were facing. We can then share David's doxology of praise as, one with Jesus Christ, we confess that our help has been in the name of the Lord, the Maker of heaven and earth.

Responding

Here are some suggestions to help with your own 'godly remembrance'. It may help to write things down as you remember.

Can you remember the pivotal events in your Christian story, such as:

- the day you first trusted the Lord Jesus?

- the time you first realised the abundance of His love?
- occasions when Scripture came alive and spoke to you?
- a time when prayer has been wonderfully answered?
- a time when the Lord's presence became very real?

Can you remember personal experiences when:

- the Lord provided for you in ways that you never expected?
- He guided you through a maze of difficult decisions?
- you struggled to forgive and He helped you?
- He gave fresh hope in a time of grief?

6
Psalm 125
Praying for Steadfastness

¹ Those who trust in the LORD are like Mount Zion,
which cannot be moved, but abides for ever.
² As the mountains surround Jerusalem,
so the LORD surrounds his people,
from this time on and for evermore.
³ For the sceptre of wickedness shall not rest
on the land allotted to the righteous,
so that the righteous may not stretch out
their hands to do wrong.
⁴ Do good, O LORD, to those who are good,
and to those who are upright in their hearts.
⁵ But those who turn aside to their own crooked ways
the LORD will lead away with evildoers.
Peace be upon Israel!

Introducing Psalm 125

The divine certainty of safety for the Lord's people (vv1-2)

The Lord's people are those who trust Him, and in that trust they know a wonderful safety and hope. The psalmist says that these pilgrims travelling together as people who trust in the Lord are as secure as Mount Zion, the destination on which they have set their sights.

The picture in verse 1 is of a city founded upon a rock. The city established by David was on a protruding ridge of limestone with steep sides all around. Those who trust in Israel's covenant Lord are promised that they are as safe as this city built on that solid foundation. Their assurance is strengthened by the fact that the temple on this outcrop of rock is the place where the Lord has promised to live eternally.[1] Promise and presence combine to give the assurance of lasting safety and divine accompaniment in the face of every threat and disaster.

The picture in verse 2 changes to that of a city surrounded by mountains. This, says the psalmist, is the way the Lord encircles His people on every side with His complete protection, both now and into the far reaches of eternity.

The pilgrims celebrate the Lord's provision of complete protection and security for all those who place their trust in Him.

Assurance is threatened by the rule of evil (v3)

The Jews in the time of Jesus had experienced more domination by foreign powers than almost any other nation in the Middle East. Over hundreds of years Canaanite, Philistine, Syrian, Assyrian, Babylonian, Persian, Seleucid and Roman forces had cruelly occupied their land. With them, they had brought slaughter, oppression, deportation, as well as the insidious influences of pagan religion and practices. The Lord's

---

[1] See also Psalm 132:13-14.

people were continually exposed to the danger of being drawn away from their trust in Him, tempted constantly to follow the ways of foreign gods. The sceptre of wickedness, symbolising authority and punishment, hung over the people of Israel. Their history sadly, was one of deserting the worship of the true and living God and turning to other gods. Scattered through their history were examples of rulers who 'did what was evil in the sight of the LORD',[2] a phrase that occurs nearly forty times in the Old Testament, starting with the rule of the Judges right through to the time of Jeremiah.

Although they knew that there was eternal security to be found in trusting their Lord, the temptation to conform to the practices and beliefs of the occupying forces repeatedly proved too much for them. The reality of evil is always present, says the psalmist, and so also is the temptation to fall under its influence. However, the Lord will set a limit to the rule of these oppressors, because in His faithfulness He will not let His people be tempted beyond that which they can endure.

A prayer for blessing when under the rule of evil (v4)

The difficulty of living faithfully under foreign domination drives the psalmist to pray for strength to stand firm when such temptations arise. The rule of wickedness is overwhelming, and love for the Lord seems to be wavering. This cry for the Lord's blessing, in the midst of an intense struggle to resist temptation, comes from a heart that is acutely aware of a growing distance from the presence and knowledge of the Lord.

---

[2] Judges 2:11; 2 Kings 24:19; Jeremiah 52:2.

It might seem as if the psalmist is bargaining with his Lord. 'If I do good, will you be good to me, Lord?' Is it a request for God to show favour to those who deserve His favour? Certainly not! The key lies in the last four words of the first part of verse 4: 'those who are good'. In the original Hebrew text, this is one word which means 'upright' and it is qualified by the second line of the verse: 'those who are upright in their hearts'. The goodness of verse 4 must be a quality that is more than skin deep!

Paraphrased, the verse might read, 'Lord, will You act in accordance with Your good nature and deliver me from the temptation to do evil; I only pray this because I depend on Your forgiveness and grace at work in my heart, the centre of my life, transforming me into the righteous person You want me to be.'

The danger of succumbing to the threat (v5a)

Now comes the dreadful realisation that a persistent yielding to temptation, combined with a determination to follow those who do evil, can carry the eternal consequences of banishment from the presence of the Lord. The verse carries the strong sense that this turning aside to evil is a definite choice. We know from Scripture that the Lord's blessing and forgiveness is eternally assured to those who obey Him with a rooted faith and trust in His promises.[3] Here, though, there seems to be the suggestion that a deliberate and wilful backsliding to 'crooked ways' can lead to exile from the Lord. We'll return to this later in the section entitled 'A warning and an assurance'.

---

[3] See also Genesis 15:6; Romans 4:2-3.

A plea for safety in the Lord (v5b)

Here is a cry from the heart that the people of God may be those who are upright in heart rather than those who choose to walk in 'the counsel of the wicked' (Psalm 1:1). The closing prayer of the psalm is that the *shalom*, the totality of the blessings of the Lord's covenant love,[4] will rest on those who continue in faithfulness to the Lord who first loved them.

Jesus and Psalm 125

It is important to understand the political situation in Judea and Galilee at the time of Jesus if we are to see how Jesus might have prayed this psalm. Herod the Great was appointed ruler in 37BC to govern the whole of Palestine as a protectorate allied to Rome and under Roman supervision. The emperor granted Herod considerable power as a convenient way of protecting the eastern fringes of his empire from attack. On Herod's death, Judea and Galilee became provincial administrative districts, governed by Herod's sons, Antipas and Archelaus. Antipas was made ruler of Galilee and Perea where he ruled until AD39. Archelaus ruled with great cruelty over Judea until AD6 when he was banished to the northern reaches of the Roman Empire and replaced by a series of Roman procurators, of whom Pontius Pilate was the sixth, governing from AD26 to AD36. Herod Antipas remained as a puppet king alongside these procurators.

Every aspect of Jewish life in Judea was treated with utter contempt by the occupying Romans, who set the tone

---

[4] See remarks on Psalm 122:6-9, 'Praying for Jerusalem', in chapter 3.

of everyday life. Jewish high priests were appointed by the procurator, who allowed the wearing of the high priestly robes only at his discretion. All religious affairs and most civil matters were controlled by the Sanhedrin, under the presidency of the high priest, who in turn was at the beck and call of the procurator. Pontius Pilate was intolerably cruel and thought nothing of ordering countless executions without trial. The Gospels describe him as harsh, imperious, cynical, selfish and contemptuous (Matthew 27:24; Luke 13:1; John 18:38). Life was wretched for the Jews under this heavy burden of domination.

The coming of Jesus Christ, the Son of God, born as a human being in this cruel and broken world, provoked both the political and spiritual forces of evil to do their worst.

> His coming brought not peace but a sword, for it was his birth that provoked the dreadful savagery of Herod against the infants of Bethlehem – and that was but the initial sign of the upheaval which the coming of the king and his kingdom meant for the kingdoms of this world.[5]

Now we can understand how Jesus might have prayed through this psalm. From the moment of His birth He lived under the sceptre of wickedness, as the 'Prince of Peace' (Isaiah 9:6) come to fulfil His Father's purposes of salvation. He suffered the everyday deprivation of living under foreign occupation alongside His fellow Jews, knowing full well that the day would come when He

[5] Thomas F Torrance, *Incarnation: The Person and Life of Christ*, ed Robert T Walker, (Downers Grove, IL: IVP Academic, 2008), p140.

would be arrested by these powers, put on trial and led out to crucifixion. As His three years of public ministry progressed, the determination of the Jewish authorities and the supporters of Herod Antipas to arrest and kill Him intensified. Evil forces were gathering in council. Battle was finally joined in the trial of Jesus before Jewish, Herodian and Roman rulers, and then in the three hours of darkness on the cross. After an intensity of conflict which we will never fully understand, 'He disarmed the rulers and authorities and made a public example of them, triumphing over them' by the cross (Colossians 2:15).

Facing this unimaginable suffering and clash of powers, Jesus remained utterly confident in the unshakeable character of His Father and His encircling love (vv1-2). He knew as He prayed the psalms that the day would come when, at the command of His Father, He would rule the nations with 'a rod of iron' (Psalm 2:9) holding 'a sceptre of equity' (Psalm 45:6). His prayer that the sceptre of wickedness would not remain over the land allotted to the righteous could only be answered as He went to the cross and carried in His own person the complete and total judgement of His Father on the sin and wickedness of this world. The psalmist's prayer (v4) was to be finally and conclusively answered in His last words on the cross, 'It is finished' (John 19:30). The sceptre of wickedness had been finally broken. The righteous rule of the kingdom of God was established at that final cry and sealed for eternity when Jesus burst from the tomb in glorious new life.

Now the promise of peace celebrated by angels at His birth was fulfilled. The militant and evil attack on His presence as King in the world was defeated. The possibility of life for eternity under the sceptre of God's righteous rule was established. By His life, death and resurrection, Jesus made the concluding prayer of this psalm a reality when He appeared to His disciples on the first Easter evening and said to them, 'Peace be with you' (John 20:21).

Reading Psalm 125 as a follower of Jesus

A warning and an assurance

We were reminded at the beginning of this chapter that the Lord encircles His people on every side with His complete protection, both now and into the far reaches of eternity (vv1-2). But in verse 5, there seems to be the suggestion that a deliberate and wilful turning aside to 'crooked ways' can lead to exile from the Lord. How do we manage this apparent contradiction? Are the Lord's people eternally secure or is there a real danger of falling away?

Scripture teaches us constantly that the Lord's covenant with His people is unshakeable, sealed eternally and permanently in Christ.[6] But there are also passages that teach us that falling away from the Lord's keeping is a real possibility.[7] How is this apparent contradiction to be explained?

Some might want to adjust the permanence of the Lord's promises, arguing that there is a real danger of falling away. Others might want to adjust the gravity of the warning passages, denying the possibility of finding

---

[6] See John 6:35-40; Romans 8:1-2; 2 Corinthians 1:20; 1 Peter 1:3-5.
[7] See Matthew 24:9-13; Luke 9:62; Hebrews 6:1-8; 10:26.

oneself outside the scope of God's salvation. Each adjustment has its problems. One diminishes the threats we face as Christians living in an evil world; the other diminishes the reality of God's promises. Vernon Grounds (1914–2010), who was chancellor of Denver Theological Seminary, wrote about the paradoxes we find in Scripture and concluded as follows: 'Very likely we are being loyal to the Bible as long as we feel upon our minds the tug of logical tension.'[8]

The apostle Paul's doxology of wonder and praise after his long exposition of the mystery of the purposes of God suggests the way forward:

> O the depth of the riches and wisdom and knowledge of God! How unsearchable are his judgements and how inscrutable his ways!
> 'For who has known the mind of the Lord?
> Or who has been his counsellor?'
> 'Or who has given a gift to him,
> to receive a gift in return?'
> For from him and through him and to him are all things. To him be the glory for ever. Amen.
> (Romans 11:33-36)

We can never expect to understand the mind, the knowledge and the purposes of our God. Inevitably there will be tensions and paradoxes that baffle our limited and fallen human understanding. Under the guidance of the

---

[8] Vernon C Grounds, 'The Postulate of Paradox', *Bulletin of the Evangelical Theological Society*, Vol 7, 7.1, 1964, p20, which can be found at biblicalstudies.org.uk/pdf/bets/vol07/7-1_grounds.pdf (accessed 14th April 2023).

Holy Spirit, we must learn to live with these, living with the prophet Isaiah's creed:

> Have you not known? Have you not heard?
> The LORD is the everlasting God,
> the Creator of the ends of the earth.
> He does not faint or grow weary;
> his understanding is unsearchable.
> (Isaiah 40:28)

Living securely in Christ

The Christian lives in Christ and prays this psalm in the name of Christ, resting in faith on the person, life and work of the incarnate Son of God. The Lord Jesus revealed fully the depth of the love of His Father and established the unsurpassed and eternal security of all who live in Him by the sheer wonder of the redemption He accomplished. The Christian is even more secure in Jesus Christ than the city of Zion was on the rock on which it was built. Every child of God in Christ is encircled by the mountains of the Lord's covenant love. The safety and certainty of that standing is, as Paul puts it, irrefutable and cannot be shaken by anything 'living or dead, angelic or demonic, today or tomorrow, high or low, thinkable or unthinkable ... because of the way that Jesus our Master has embraced us' (Romans 8:38-39, *The Message*). Our praying must always celebrate and express a deep thankfulness for the security of our position in Christ, bought at such cost and sacrifice.

As the psalmist admits in verse 3, the Lord's people are faced every day with the dark reality of evil which remains over this world.[9] John Goldingay's analysis is perceptive:

> In today's religion/culture wars, the faithless are winning and have led the faithful to put their hands to wickedness in the sense that church culture like secular culture is dominated by money, possession, size, individualism, family breakdown, narcissism, overwork and an acceptance of the gulf between rich and poor.[10]

It is far too easy to allow ourselves to be dominated and enslaved by the culture and fashions of this world. In our own individual lives, we face the temptations hurled at us incessantly by the evil one, who prowls around like a roaring lion with the single aim of destroying us (1 Peter 5:8). The struggle to keep the faith and run with endurance can be hard at times. Psalm 125 is a reminder as well as a prayer for pilgrims who need to know that they are utterly secure in the rock-like and encircling love of the Lord. Such assurance is the birthright of every child of God.[11]

The psalm concludes on a high point with the words, 'Peace be upon Israel!' We are taken again to the evening of the day of Christ's resurrection and to the room where the disciples had locked themselves away 'for fear of the Jews'. The risen Christ came and stood among them, greeting them with the same words: 'Peace be with you'

---

[9] 1 John 5:19.

[10] John Goldingay, *Psalms: Volume 3: Psalms 90-150* (Grand Rapids, MI: Baker Academic, 2008), p488.

[11] 1 Peter 1:3-9.

(John 20:19-20). He had formerly conferred on them a kingdom (Luke 22:29), and now as the King of that kingdom He blessed them with the *shalom* of God, the totality of the blessings of the Lord's covenant love. No doubt remained for those disciples, and there is no doubt for all who follow them that the psalmist's prayer for the Lord to do good is fully answered in Jesus Christ. We have been blessed 'in Christ with every spiritual blessing' (Ephesians 1:3).

Responding

'Every step taken … is to be a step forward in our growth in Christ.' The apostle James wrote, 'Whenever you face trials of any kind, consider it nothing but joy, because you know that the testing of your faith produces endurance' (James 1:2-3). How do you feel when you read this?

What are the influences that can undermine our Christian faith today?

Psalm 125 reminds me that I am 'utterly secure in the rock-like and encircling love of the Lord. Such assurance is the birthright of every child of God'. Is there anything that prevents that for me? How can I discover and live in that security?

7
Psalm 126
Laughter and Tears

¹ When the LORD restored the fortunes of Zion,
we were like those who dream.
² Then our mouth was filled with laughter,
and our tongue with shouts of joy;
then it was said among the nations,
'The LORD has done great things for them.'
³ The LORD has done great things for us,
and we rejoiced.
⁴ Restore our fortunes, O LORD,
like the watercourses in the Negeb.
⁵ May those who sow in tears
reap with shouts of joy.
⁶ Those who go out weeping,
bearing the seed for sowing,
shall come home with shouts of joy,
carrying their sheaves.

Introducing Psalm 126

Psalm 126 remembers the harrowing experience of captivity, an experience so dreadful that release can only bring uncontrolled laughter and ecstatic joy. It is about the Lord who acts to release His people from the struggles of life and their longing for freedom and hope, themes echoed in the opening verses of Peter's first epistle:

> Blessed be the God and Father of our Lord Jesus Christ! By his great mercy he has given us a new birth into a living hope through the resurrection of Jesus Christ from the dead, and into an inheritance that is imperishable, undefiled, and unfading, kept in heaven for you, who are being protected by the power of God through faith for a salvation ready to be revealed in the last time. In this you rejoice, even if now for a little while you have had to suffer various trials, so that the genuineness of your faith – being more precious than gold that, though perishable, is tested by fire – may be found to result in praise and glory and honour when Jesus Christ is revealed. Although you have not seen him, you love him; and even though you do not see him now, you believe in him and rejoice with an indescribable and glorious joy, for you are receiving the outcome of your faith, the salvation of your souls.
> (1 Peter 1:3-9)

The Lord has acted (vv1-3)

The deliverance described at the start of the psalm is usually understood to be the return of Jewish exiles from captivity in Babylon to Jerusalem. When Jerusalem had been destroyed by the Babylonians in 597BC, the majority of the inhabitants of the land were taken into exile in Babylon. The depths of pain and distress brought by enemy conquest and captivity are described vividly by Jeremiah and Ezekiel when they speak of terror, fear, calamity and violence. The Jewish exiles' experience in Babylon was one of agonising torment and tears which continued for more than forty years.[1] But in 538BC, the Persian emperor, Cyrus the Great, conquered Babylon. He issued an immediate edict giving permission for all captive people in his empire to return to their homelands. Ezra, the scribe, records this momentous declaration in the opening verses of his book.[2] Groups of exiled Jews gradually returned to Jerusalem and the surrounding towns, rebuilding their homes and restoring their lands to productivity. Ezra recollects the people assembling in Jerusalem soon after their return to celebrate the laying of the foundations of the new temple. It was an occasion of great rejoicing, but one that brought memories flooding back:

> Many of the priests and Levites and heads of families, old people who had seen the first house on its foundations, wept with a loud voice when they saw this house, though many shouted aloud for joy, so that the people could not distinguish the sound of the joyful shout from the sound of the people's weeping, for the people shouted so loudly that the sound was heard far away.
> (Ezra 3:12-13)

The laments and praises of the people were heard far and wide. As well as tears, the day brought untold happiness as the people laughed for joy and sang songs of praise to

---

[1] Psalm 137; Jeremiah 30:4-7; Ezekiel 7.
[2] Ezra 1:1-4.

the Lord who had done such wonderful things for them. Their sheer elation could not be silenced.

This release from captivity in Babylon was one of many episodes in the history of the Lord's people when He acted dramatically to save them. Written into the DNA of every Jew was the Lord's miraculous deliverance of His people from their captivity in Egypt on the first Passover night. The song they sang on the eastern shores of the Red Sea after the destruction of Pharaoh's army (Exodus 15:1-18) has similarities to Psalm 126 as the fleeing Children of Israel sing with unrestrained joy about the Lord's mighty act of salvation, one seen by the surrounding nations. Psalm 126 could also describe the dreadful siege of Jerusalem in 722BC by Sennacherib, the Assyrian king. The capitulation and retreat by night of his terrorising army following King Hezekiah's prayer could only have been the result of the Lord's dramatic intervention and, similarly, Hezekiah was 'exalted in the sight of all nations' (2 Chronicles 32:23).[3]

But the words of verse 1 do not just relate to the release of the Lord's people from captivity in Babylon. Alec Motyer translates the verse as follows: 'When Yahweh brought back the banishment of Zion we were like people dreaming.' The word translated 'banishment', he says, 'could refer to any experience of alienation from Yahweh'.[4] That sense of exile from the Lord is an experience often referred to by the psalmists.[5] When the Lord brings His

---

[3] The story is told in 2 Kings 18-19 and 2 Chronicles 32.

[4] Alec Motyer, *Psalms by the Day: A New Devotional Translation* (Fearn, Tain: Christian Focus Publications, 2016), p375.

[5] For example: Psalm 6; 10; 31; 63; 84.

people back to Himself, there is inexpressible joy and laughter instead of tears and hopelessness. The reality of this joy only serves to emphasise the intensity of the darkness experienced as a result of alienation from the Lord.

Whether it is release from political captivity or restoration to fellowship with the Lord, it was like finding that something dreamt about was actually true. As John Goldingay puts it, 'we pinched ourselves to check that we were awake and found we were'.[6] The Lord had saved His people. And there is more to the word 'dream' (v1), as Goldingay suggests. It can also mean a return to health and strength after a time of sickness. As well as saving His people, the Lord was restoring them to wholeness. Both meanings, taken together, add richness to the verse. The psalmist's description of the joy and laughter of verse 2 brought about by the Lord's intervention was so exuberant that it could only be repeated in verse 3. Such was the wonder and praise of their worship.

To summarise, the psalmist in verses 1-3 is recalling the wonder of the Lord's saving acts throughout His people's history. He is recalling times of returning to the Lord's presence after periods of alienation and other times of brokenness. Such events brought elation and overwhelming happiness to His people. They could not help but laugh for joy and sing songs of praise to the Lord. He has acted for them in the past and He will do wonderful things for them in the future. Their joy and praise is heard and spoken about by all those around who

---

[6] Goldingay, *Psalms: Volume 3: Psalms 90-150*, p492.

recognise the intervention of God in the lives of His people.

The Lord will act (vv4-6)

We are brought back to earth with a bump in verse 4! The psalmist's prayer could be paraphrased, 'Things are certainly not so good for the Lord's people now. Many still need to return. Would that things were like they once were! Act again as You did in the past, Lord. Bring us to trust You in the dryness of this season, realising that the day will come when we see You speaking and acting again in power.'

Some of the words used are the same as in verse 1, but there is a different slant. Celebration has gone now, only to be replaced by a heartfelt pleading that the Lord will restore His people. Many are still in exile far from home; many know that they are far from the Lord; few have seen Him at work in their lives; all long to be restored to wholeness. Their lives, both physical and spiritual, are dry and they cry out for the Lord to act. A dramatic transformation is needed, akin to the refreshment of rain in the Negeb, the semi-desert region of southern Israel, bringing green grass and flowers to flourish in previously arid places. How is this to happen?

The rest of the psalm (vv5-6) answers that question. It is not with the dramatic intervention of the Lord described at the beginning of the psalm. The cure for such dryness of spirit will only happen as the one who prays cooperates with the One who listens. The picture is painted of a farming community. There will be weeping and tears as the seed is carried and sown; there will be the inevitable wait for the growth of the seed and ripening of the grain.

The wait, sometimes seemingly interminable, will require persistent faith and trust in the Lord of the harvest. But harvest there will be! It is certain because prayer has been made to the promise-keeping Lord of steadfast love. When it comes there will be a harvest to reap and to bring home. There will be songs of joy again!

Perhaps the promise of the Lord to Amos was in the mind of the psalmist as he wrote these concluding verses:

> The time is surely coming, says the LORD,
> when the one who ploughs shall overtake the one who reaps,
> and the treader of grapes the one who sows the seed;
> the mountains shall drip sweet wine,
> and all the hills shall flow with it.
> I will restore the fortunes of my people Israel,
> and they shall rebuild the ruined cities and inhabit them;
> they shall plant vineyards and drink their wine,
> and they shall make gardens and eat their fruit.
> (Amos 9:13-14)

Those who are sent out by the Lord of the harvest to labour in His harvest field, often with great hardship, will experience the same joy and laughter described by the psalmist. Tears of hard, unremitting labour will be replaced by songs of triumphant joy. The Lord has acted to save and restore in the past, and even though the present may be dark and threatening, the psalmist trusts Him to act and save in the future.

Jesus and Psalm 126

Jesus came to release His people from captivity

In the months preceding and following the birth of Jesus Christ, faithful servants of the Lord spoke of the fact that here was the One who was coming to deliver and redeem His people from captivity. Before Jesus was born, Zechariah, the father of John the Baptist, was filled with the Holy Spirit and declared that his promised son, John, would prepare the way for the One who would deliver His people from the oppression and fear of their enemies.[7]

Simeon was a righteous and devout man living in Jerusalem. The Lord had told him that he would not die before he had seen the Messiah. Blessing God, he took the infant Jesus in his arms and spoke of the salvation that this child would bring to both Jews and Gentiles. Anna, the prophetess who lived and prayed constantly in the temple, saw Joseph and Mary with Jesus. Realising just who this infant was, she gave thanks to God! She could not help but speak about this child to all who longed to see the coming Messiah.[8]

At this time, there was a simmering expectation that the Messiah was about to come and deliver the oppressed Jews from Roman domination. Zechariah's prophecy, Simeon's song and the words of Anna were spoken into the cauldron of this anticipation. The Redeemer who was about to come and save His people was Jesus.

After the start of His public ministry, Jesus went to Nazareth and taught in the synagogue. His text spoke of

---

[7] Luke 1:67-79.
[8] Luke 2:22-38.

deliverance for those who were held captive. More was to come as He announced to the listening congregation that He was actually the One who would bring about that deliverance. The prophets had repeatedly spoken of Israel's release in the days to come.

Now, said Jesus, 'The Spirit of the Lord is upon me.' He was the One who would bring this prophecy to its fulfilment (Luke 4:16-21).

Jesus Christ, Son of God, the anointed Servant of the Lord, had arrived in order to bring release from captivity in fulfilment of the Messianic prophecies of the Old Testament.

Jesus defined the captivity in which all people are held

Speaking in the temple, Jesus came under increasing opposition from the Jews to whom He spoke. However, John recounts that when some of them said they believed in Him, Jesus set out to test the genuineness of their belief:

> Then Jesus said to the Jews who had believed in him, 'If you continue in my word, you are truly my disciples; and you will know the truth, and the truth will make you free.' They answered him, 'We are descendants of Abraham and have never been slaves to anyone. What do you mean by saying, "You will be made free"?'
> (John 8:31-33)

Jesus told them that if they remained steadfast to His teaching, they would discover the truth that would set them free. They replied indignantly, saying that they had always been free and that they had never been held in slavery, managing somehow to ignore their long history of oppression and captivity under Egypt, Assyria, Babylon, Greece, Syria and now Rome. The defining answer Jesus then gave them revealed the devastating nature of the captivity in which all men and women live: Jesus answered them, 'Very truly, I tell you, everyone who commits sin is a slave to sin' (John 8:34).[9] There is a universal captivity from which there is no release unless the truth revealed in Jesus is known and accepted. It was a momentous claim. Jesus was saying that if we recognise that all truth is in Jesus and we do nothing about it, we are slaves to sin. Conversely, He says that if you are completely committed to His words and the truth about Him, you will be free. He is truth and only He can release us from our captivity to sin.

Paul talked about the fact that all are held in slavery to sin, and he amplified that by stating that this slavery is the same as being spiritually dead.[10] It is a captivity which dulls the human spirit and closes the eyes and sensitivities of men and women to the holiness and love of the Lord.

The way to freedom from this captivity to sin was to be secured through the cross. Speaking later in the temple, Jesus stated that freedom and abundance of life was only possible as He, the good Shepherd, laid down His life for the sheep. He would lay down His life and 'take it up again' (John 10:7-18).

---

[9] Jesus underlined the importance of this statement by preceding it with the words, 'Very truly,' one of twenty-five occasions in John's Gospel where He used this formula.
[10] Romans 6:15-23; Ephesians 2:1-9.

Jesus was made a captive to free those in captivity to sin

The anger of the Jewish authorities grew by the day, and with it their determination to get rid of this teacher. The One who came to bring release and freedom to men and women who were captive to sin became a captive Himself. After the Last Supper and His intercession in Gethsemane, an armed band of soldiers accompanied by Pharisees and officers from the chief priests arrested and bound Jesus, marching Him off to the high priest's house. Jesus made it clear that His captivity was voluntary. At any time He could have called on armies of angels to rescue Him.[11] It was in loving obedience to His Father's will that He laid down His life, becoming imprisoned by sinful men in order to bring freedom to those bound in captivity by sin.

On that cross, Jesus, the man who was God, died. Joseph of Arimathea, with the help of Nicodemus, carried the body of Jesus to a tomb which had never been used, and laid him there. The mystery of the hours during which the dead and wounded body of Jesus lay in the tomb is beyond any human understanding:

> The chasm that separates man from God in the very existence of sinful man is the black abyss of hell. And Christ descended into that hell in order to redeem. He the mediator descended into the black pit of human alienation from God in order to save. In his own incarnate person he united man and God and bore the guilt of man before the presence of God. It is because the godly majesty of God, the

---

[11] Matthew 26:53.

righteous law of God, the holy love of God, stands inexorably in the path between mankind and God that the gravity of the situation is infinite. It is such that God and only God himself can deal with it, and only God in infinite anguish.[12]

We can only stand as 'those who dream', amazed at the mystery of godliness as the One who was utterly free from before the foundation of the world is bound in the captivity of death so that He might free those who all their lives have been captive to sin.[13]

In allowing Himself to be imprisoned by the cross and death, Jesus knew that He was held in the loving will of His Father. His experience was beyond our human fathoming, but security was possible even in that depth of suffering because He could say to His Father:

> For you do not give me up to Sheol,
> or let your faithful one see the Pit.
> You show me the path of life.
> In your presence there is fullness of joy;
> in your right hand are pleasures for evermore.
> (Psalm 16:10-11)

It was on the third day that God raised Jesus up from the prison of death. The joy of that resurrection morning was immeasurable. The Son of God was released from His exile, and with Him all who had trusted and were to trust in His word.[14] The celebrations resounded throughout

---

[12] Torrance, *Incarnation*, p255.

[13] See Hebrews 2:14-15.

[14] John 8:36.

heaven and earth as the risen Lord Jesus ascended to the right hand of the Father. From that seat of all authority and power, Jesus Christ sent the Holy Spirit to live with His followers, made righteous in Christ but needing that Divine Advocacy in their struggles with temptation and attacks from the evil one. Their path of tearful sowing leads only to 'shouts of joy' (v2) when they arrive where Jesus is and see His glory.[15] Exile will be past and Christ 'will himself restore, support, strengthen, and establish you' (1 Peter 5:10).

Reading Psalm 126 as a follower of Jesus

Life seated with Christ (vv1-3)

Every follower of Jesus Christ has experienced this miraculous release from captivity that the psalmist talks about, delivered by the Father 'from the power of darkness and transferred … into the kingdom of his beloved Son, in whom we have redemption, the forgiveness of sins' (Colossians 1:13–14). Formerly under the sentence of death because of our slavery to the bondage of sin, we have been raised to life with Christ (we could never have even dreamt this), and the old sentence of death has been cancelled and nailed to the cross of Christ.[16]

God acted dramatically in Christ to bring His people back from a dreadful and hopeless life far from Himself. In Christ, we have come home and our hearts respond in praise and worship as we realise the enormity of all that

---

[15] John 17:24.
[16] Colossians 2:13-15.

has been achieved for us. Weeping has been turned into laughter, imprisonment to freedom and despair to joy as we realise the security and deliverance we have in Christ as redeemed people released from captivity:

> God rescues us from the present evil age by joining us to Christ by the Spirit. We are co-crucified with Christ, co-resurrected, and now brought into the new age along with Christ to enjoy the life of God. We now participate in the coming age of resurrection and heavenly life. Just as Christ is now already exalted, so we are too![17]

Life in the here and now (vv4-6)

Although the future reality of the new creation is part of our inheritance now as we are joined to Christ by the Holy Spirit, we still live our lives in the old creation, where sin reigns and evil powers hold sway. We have to learn to live in the present as well as hold on to the future.

The desert can be the experience of many Christians, and the dryness of that desert journey and the longing for the refreshment of the Holy Spirit is expressed vividly in verse 4 of the psalm. The Lord seems absent in the heat of the day, and there are few markers to show us the way. Exhausted and parched, we cry out for rain in the desert experiences of our lives. This was David's experience recounted in Psalm 63.

Many in church leadership and mission at home or overseas have toiled for years and seen little fruit.

---

[17] Timothy G Gombis, *The Drama of Ephesians, Participating in the Triumph of God* (Downers Grove, InterVarsity Press, 2010), p95.

Christians seeking to reap a harvest for Christ in the family, the community or the workplace often see few answers to their prayers. But ministry in leadership and commitment to mission in our communities and places of work will certainly be rewarded. The message of this psalm is for faithful servants of Christ who are promised a reward of joy in God's time.

George Müller (1805–98) was the founder of several children's orphanages in nineteenth-century England, organising them and funding them only through prayer. Year after year, he trusted the Lord to provide everything for the orphans in his care, and God never failed to supply their needs. But there was one prayer of Müller's that remained unanswered. For more than sixty-three years, Müller prayed that a friend of his would become a Christian. Although other prayers were answered, this one remained unanswered: his friend refused to trust Christ. Even as Müller died, his prayer remained unanswered. But then there was an answer. His friend made the decision to accept Christ before Müller's funeral. The promise of this psalm had been honoured!

When my wife and I have gone through desert times of waiting for God to answer our prayers, we have found great encouragement in the story that Darrell Johnson tells in his book about the Lord's Prayer:

> Four days before Christmas of 2000 our then 18-year-old son Alex, whom we had adopted six years earlier from an orphanage in Moscow, went hiking with a group of friends in the mountains just north of Los Angeles. They were making their way along a loose rock slope when the rocks gave way, and

Alex slid down the slope and then over a 120-foot cliff. When the rescue team arrived some 40 minutes later, the helicopter pilot said he was sure Alex was dead – too much blood had flowed from his head for him to be alive. But when two of the paramedics got to him they found a pulse, and quickly rushed him to the trauma center in Pasadena. By the time Sharon and I made it to the hospital, Alex was already in a coma and attached to life-support systems. The neurosurgeons could not say whether Alex would live. If he made it until Christmas Eve then there was hope he would recover. Even if he survived, the doctors would not say what kind of life he would have.

On the night before Christmas Eve, as I drove home from having spent the day in the ICU, I heard the following words, which I keep in my journal:

Things are not as they seem. In your life. In your son's life. In your wife's life. In the lives of your other children. In the lives of other patients in ICU. Things are not as they seem. There is more going on than meets the un-aided senses. There is a God. A Living God. A good God. A faithful God. A powerful God. A reigning God. An ever-present God. There is never a time when this God is not good. There is never a time when this God is not faithful. There is never a time when this God is not powerful. There is never a time when the God of the Bible is not on the throne of the universe. There is never a time when the God

we meet in Jesus is not present. It is a promise:
'I will never leave you or forsake you.'[18]

These words which Darrell Johnson heard from the Lord and wrote in his journal have been a great source of strength to my wife and myself as we have waited, sometimes for years, for God's answers to our prayers.

There is toil that seems unrewarded and prayer that seems in vain. The message of this psalm, though, is one of profound hope. Our experience of captivity will one day become a fact of the past. What we believe by faith will become a reality.

> We will be holy and blameless ... freed from our distorted, bound, compromised and temporal existences into a restored, liberated, unimpaired and eternal existence in Christ.[19]

Responding

Captivity to sin is a universal but dreadful fact. Jesus said, 'If you continue in my word, you are truly my disciples; and you will know the truth, and the truth will make you free' (John 8:31-32). What do you think it means to abide in His Word?

The experience of spiritual dryness is very common, made worse by the guilt accompanying it, as we admit

---

[18] Johnson, *Fifty-Seven Words that Change the World*, pp98-99. Darrell Johnson adds a note (p100): 'Alex, I am grateful to report, lived and is making a remarkable recovery. And he loves the Father. *That* is the miracle.' (Used with the author's permission.)

[19] Marcus Peter Johnson, *One with Christ: An Evangelical Theology of Salvation* (Wheaton, IL: Crossway, 2013), p187.

that we cannot love the Lord as we did before. Psalms 31 and 63 speak about similar times in David's life. How might we help someone we know who is currently suffering an emptiness or dryness of faith?

Note: There is a short and very helpful booklet entitled *Spiritual Dryness* by Walter Trobisch. It was published by InterVarsity Press in 1970 but sadly it is no longer in print. It is available from secondhand booksellers.

Reading Psalms 127 and 128

Psalms 127 and 128 are Wisdom Psalms, both covering the same subject but from different standpoints. They have the typical characteristics of the Wisdom books of the Old Testament (Job, Proverbs and Ecclesiastes), which can be summarised as follows:

- The fundamental principle that 'the fear of the LORD is the beginning of wisdom' (Psalm 111:10; see also Proverbs 1:7; 9:10).
- The fundamental belief that the Lord created and orders all things in His sovereignty (Proverbs 3:19-20).
- We can choose either to walk the way of wisdom which leads to life, or to walk the way of vanity and foolishness which leads to death (Proverbs 8:32-36).
- The Lord rewards those who obey His law and punishes those who transgress it (Psalm 34:11-16; Proverbs 1:20-33).
- The person who fears the Lord is blessed. Life will be as God intended and will be lived in peace in the land God gave to His people (Psalm 37:3-6).

There is a constant tension in the Wisdom literature of the Old Testament between what is ideal and the everyday experiences of life, which is to be lived in the fear of the Lord and according to His Law. Illustrations from nature are frequently used as well as pithy sayings about rewards and retribution. A clear line is drawn between those who choose to trust in the Lord and those who refuse to acknowledge Him. Blessings result from obedience to the commands of the Lord; curses, similar to those pronounced after sin had entered Eden, are the result of disobedience.[1]

Four keys to understanding Psalm 127 and 128

The first key to understanding these psalms is the phrase 'the fear of the LORD'. It means a life lived in submissive obedience to the Lord who has shown Himself to us as a holy and loving God. Such a life is both happy and blessed by God. Psalm 127 paints a picture of life without the fear of the Lord (vv1-2), before stating what would be different if the fear of the Lord became a central feature of life (vv3-5). Psalm 128 paints a picture of life lived with the fear of the Lord (vv1-4) before describing the blessings accompanying such a life (vv5-6).

Second, it is helpful to understand that there are different Hebrew words for 'blessed' in these psalms. The first word implies that those who live in the fear of the Lord are truly happy (127:5 and 128:1-2). The second word (128:4-5) implies that blessing is a gift bestowed by the Lord. The New Revised Standard Version (Anglicised) translation of Psalms 127 and 128 distinguishes clearly between these two words.

Third, the Hebrew word translated 'house' in 127:1 and 128:3 covers a broad range of meanings, including a home,

---

[1] This typical Wisdom teaching about reward and retribution is partially derived from Moses' final address to the Children of Israel in Deuteronomy 27–28 (especially 28:1-24).

a family, a dwelling place, a dynasty (such as 'the house of David') or a whole nation (such as 'the house of Israel').[2] We must avoid interpreting this word and these two psalms according to the Western understanding of the nuclear family. The Old Testament concept of the family consisted of several generations of families related by blood and marriage, including the place where they lived. As well as its land, houses, fields and livestock, such a community could consist of anything from fifty to 100 people, possibly including:

> Husband and wife, their children (and if their sons were married, their wives and children), the husband's parents, the husband's brothers and their families, the husband's unmarried sisters, and other relatives … Besides those related by blood or marriage, the household would include servants and slaves, guests (who were bound to the family by the obligations of hospitality), and sojourners (aliens resident in the household and under its ongoing protection, often employees of the household).[3]

I have chosen to use the words 'household' and 'community' to cover the breadth of the word used in 127:1 and 128:3.

---

[2] 1 Samuel 20:16; Isaiah 5:7.

[3] Brenda B Colijn, 'Families in the Bible: A Brief Survey', *Ashland Theological Journal*, 36:1, 2004, p73, biblicalstudies.org.uk/pdf/ashland_theological_journal/36-1_073.pdf (accessed 14th April 2023).

Fourth, Psalms 127 and 128 are difficult to appreciate when we approach them from the standpoint of Western life today. We enjoy a measure of safety, peace and freedom, protected by good health services and legal systems. The world of the psalmist was very different, with repeated threats of war, famine, injustice, illness and death.

8
Psalm 127
Futility and Happiness
(The first of two Wisdom Psalms)

¹ Unless the LORD builds the house,
those who build it labour in vain.
Unless the LORD guards the city,
the guard keeps watch in vain.
² It is in vain that you rise up early
and go late to rest,
eating the bread of anxious toil;
for he gives sleep to his beloved.
³ Sons are indeed a heritage from the LORD,
the fruit of the womb a reward.
⁴ Like arrows in the hand of a warrior
are the sons of one's youth.
⁵ Happy is the man who has
his quiver full of them.
He shall not be put to shame
when he speaks with his enemies in the gate.

Introducing Psalm 127

The futility of life without the fear of the Lord (vv1-2)

Three proverbs open this section with a three-fold repetition of the phrase 'in vain'. The psalmist powerfully drives home the point that life lived without trust in the Lord is futile:

> Build a community without the Lord:
> Useless!
> Guard where you live without the Lord:
> Useless!
> Work all hours without trusting the Lord:
> Useless!

If we attempt to build a secure and well-provisioned community in our own strength and for our own ends, then all our efforts are in vain. Every detail of our lives, says the psalmist, must be developed with total trust in the Lord's sovereign care and obedience to His commands. To do otherwise is like receiving a priceless gift but using it with no regard for the maker's plans or instructions. It ends in futility. Anxiously toiling from early morning to late evening with our feet stepping endlessly on the treadmill of life is to regard 'the paltry pennies and miserable crumbs more highly than the hands that bestow them'.[1] The Lord is eager to give us infinitely greater blessings and abundance than all the everyday needs we spend so much time worrying about. When we trust in the One who has proclaimed His sovereignty over the totality

---

[1] Thielicke, *Life Can Begin Again*, p130.

of our lives, it brings the blessings of a good and manageable work–life balance and restful sleep.

The happiness that is brought by trusting in the Lord (vv3-5)

The three proverbs of verses 1-2 are followed by two more proverbs (vv3-4) and a commendation (v5).

Acknowledging the Lord's sovereignty brings the realisation that the children and young people in our communities are an inheritance from the Lord given to enrich our lives. They are to be brought up trusting in Him, distinguishing between right and wrong and making wise decisions.

As these young people grow in maturity and faith, they can bring increasing support and strength to those who nurtured them. The arrows of verse 4 are biblical symbols of strength. To receive faith-filled support and guidance from these young folk is akin to having a quiver full of powerful arrows: a gift to the community and a strong defence in any time of trouble. They will ensure the continuance of the family, its name and its land, one of the blessings promised by Moses.[2] The psalmist makes it quite clear that the stability of a community depends on its response to the lessons of the sad pictures he has painted in his opening verses.

Jesus and Psalm 127

The whole of Jesus' life was a confirmation of the truth of the opening verses of this psalm. He submitted in perfect trust and obedience to the will of His heavenly Father in

---

[2] Deuteronomy 28:1-14.

every decision taken, every word spoken and every deed done. When the Jews were seeking to kill Him, He told them 'Very truly, I tell you, the Son can do nothing on his own, but only what he sees the Father doing; for whatever the Father does, the Son does likewise' (John 5:19). When Jesus came to Jerusalem for the last time, He cried out, 'I have not spoken on my own, but the Father who sent me has himself given me a commandment about what to say and what to speak' (John 12:49). Then, after gathering with His disciples, 'he went forth to Gethsemane and to the cross, where in high priestly intercession and sacrifice he fulfilled in deed and in death the prayer of his whole incarnate life, the prayer of obedience, "Not my will, but thine be done."'[3]

A life of perfect trust, obedience and submission to His Father led Jesus to the cross, where His sacrifice achieved an immeasurably great salvation for us all. He made it possible for life to be lived in abundant usefulness rather than the uselessness described in verses 1 and 2.

Talking with His disciples before His arrest, He echoed those two verses again as He said to His disciples, 'Apart from me you can do nothing' (John 15:5). Unless they remained in Christ, nothing whatever (the original is reinforced with a double negative) could be achieved. To live in Christ, abiding (or remaining[4]) in Him, meant trusting Him, knowing Him, living in fellowship with Him and responding obediently to His words. Unless this was true, He told them, all their efforts were in vain,

---

[3] Torrance, *Incarnation*, pp120-121.
[4] NIVUK.

useless, like a dead branch fit only to be 'thrown into the fire, and burned' (John 15:6).

Later that evening, Jesus prayed for His disciples and all who would believe in Him through their witness: 'Father, I desire that those also, whom you have given me, may be with me where I am, to see my glory, which you have given me because you loved me before the foundation of the world' (John 17:24). The prayer of Jesus was that the destiny of those given to Him by His Father would be eternally secured.

Jesus had spoken before about this when He said to the crowd who sought and found Him after the feeding of the 5,000:

> Everything that the Father gives me will come to me, and anyone who comes to me I will never drive away; for I have come down from heaven, not to do my own will, but the will of him who sent me. And this is the will of him who sent me, that I should lose nothing of all that he has given me, but raise it up on the last day. This is indeed the will of my Father, that all who see the Son and believe in him may have eternal life; and I will raise them up on the last day.'
> (John 6:37-40)

That promise of Jesus was assured through the prayer of Jesus as He fulfilled His Father's purpose, 'bringing many sons and daughters to glory' (Hebrews 2:10, NIVUK). These children were the heritage of Jesus, a gift from His Father and He was 'not ashamed to call them brothers and sisters' (Hebrews 2:11, NIVUK). The writer of the epistle to the Hebrews goes further. Bringing them with Him, Jesus says to the Father, 'Here am I and the children whom God has given me' (Hebrews 2:13). It is as if He stands at the gate of heaven[5] with His forgiven and redeemed family, proclaiming that He has returned to heaven victoriously with those given to Him by the Father. His prayer that they might be with Him where He is and see His glory has been and will be fully answered![6] They are 'to be His joint-heirs; reigning with Him on His throne, sharing His unsearchable riches and His everlasting reign'.[7]

Reading Psalm 127 as a follower of Jesus

Acknowledging the Lord in everything (vv1-2)

There is an assumption in today's society that you can do or achieve anything you want as long as you set your mind to it. Our efforts to build our own security, gathering wealth and success by working harder than we have ever worked before become the key to making a success of our lives.

Psalm 127 gives the lie to this way of thinking and living. We are not the epicentre of our own lives and activities.

> Relentless compulsive work habits ('the bread of anxious toil') which our society rewards and admires are seen as a sign of weak faith and

---

[5] See Psalm 127:5.

[6] John 17:24.

[7] F B Meyer, *The Way into the Holiest: Expositions of the Epistle to the Hebrews* (London: Oliphants, 1968), p33.

assertive pride, as if God could not be trusted to accomplish his will, as if we could rearrange the universe by our own efforts.[8]

There is One greater, who created us and the universe in which we live, One whose will is infinitely greater than our decisions or ambitions. Ben Sira, the author of the apocryphal book of Ecclesiasticus, was a scribe who studied Jewish law and beliefs in Palestine around 180–175BC. He said that when we have said everything we could say about the Lord, we still fall short:

> Let the final word be: 'He is the all.'
> Where can we find the strength to praise him?
> For he is greater than all his works.
> Awesome is the Lord and very great,
> and marvellous is his power.
> Glorify the Lord and exalt him as much as you can,
> for he surpasses even that.
> When you exalt him, summon all your strength,
> and do not grow weary, for you cannot praise him enough.
> Who has seen him and can describe him?
> Or who can extol him as he is?
> (Ecclesiasticus 43:27-31)

The sheer majesty, authority, glory and power of the Lord demand that we acknowledge Him in everything, submitting to Him and seeking His guidance in all our decisions. To do less than this, says the psalmist, brings failure in spite of our best efforts; it will be 'useless'.

---

[8] Peterson, *A Long Obedience in the Same Direction*, p106.

Continually rising early to get more work done and coming home late because there was even more work to be done is anxious toil. The Lord knows what we need; He will provide. When we trust that He knows, then we can sleep peacefully!

Every possession that we own, from pennies to property, is given to us on trust from the Lord. Every decision we take is to be directed by the Lord, and every day of our life is a gift from the Lord. To experience today's provision by the Lord as we trust Him should lead us to trust Him for tomorrow. We suffer, however, from very short memories! Learning from His Word should instruct us, but we are slow pupils!

The heritage of children (vv3-5)

Before we can apply these verses to life today, we must understand what they meant in the time of the psalmist. The word 'heritage' (or 'inheritance'), referring here to children, is the same word used in the Old Testament to refer to the inheritance of the land given to Israel by the Lord. In other words, the land where they lived and the children in their households were both to be seen as outright gifts.

The same is true for us. These verses teach us that our children and our young people are gifted to us from the Lord and they must always be recognised and honoured as such.

Every relationship in our households, communities and churches is precious, but none more than our relationships with our children and young people. They are to be guarded and prayed for, given to us as an inheritance and reward from the Lord, who invites us to join with Him in the continuance of His creation and people. The pastoral care of church members over the years has convinced me that, more often than not, children and young people come to faith in Christ through the prayers of those close to them, either in their families or in the Christian community. The prayers of Christians with responsibilities for children and young people are incalculable in their value. Speaking with adult church members, I have often asked the question, 'How did you become a Christian?' Wonderfully, but perhaps unsurprisingly, the answer has so often been the discovery that parents, godparents, grandparents, Sunday school teachers or youth workers were praying for them. There is no better place for the growth of Christian faith in children and young people than the Christian community committed to them by example and in prayer.

The mention of 'arrows' (vv4-5) is a confirmation of the strength and encouragement that these young people bring as they grow to maturity in Christ and take up leadership in their communities and churches.

Responding

What things do you worry most about? Why do you think it is easier to worry rather than trust?

Do you have the assurance that God is your Father? What does Jesus say in Matthew 6:25-34 about what this might mean for you?

Write down the names of two or three children or young people you want to pray for regularly. Psalm 78:1-8 might help you as you pray for them.

9
Psalm 128
The Fear of the Lord
(The second of two Wisdom Psalms)

¹*Happy is everyone who fears the LORD,*
who walks in his ways.
² *You shall eat the fruit of the labour of your hands;*
you shall be happy, and it shall go well with you.
³ *Your wife will be like a fruitful vine*
within your house;
your children will be like olive shoots
around your table.
⁴ *Thus shall the man be blessed*
who fears the LORD.
⁵ *The LORD bless you from Zion.*
May you see the prosperity of Jerusalem
all the days of your life.
⁶ *May you see your children's children.*
Peace be upon Israel!

Introducing Psalm 128

Whereas Psalm 127 started with three proverbs about futility, Psalm 128 starts on a far more positive note by stating an ideal in a style typical of Old Testament Wisdom literature (vv1-4). The section begins and ends with the phrase 'who fears the LORD'. Those who frame their lives like this, according to the author of this 'Wisdom' psalm, will know happiness and contentment in their work, in their personal lives and in their household relationships. The second half (vv5-6) is a prayer for the blessing of the Lord.

Fearing the Lord (vv1-4)

The fear of the Lord is the essential response of the Lord's people to His covenant made with them at Mount Sinai. In Deuteronomy 5, Moses reminded the Children of Israel about that encounter with the Lord. How were they to respond? They were to 'fear the LORD' (Deuteronomy 6:1-2). This central theme of Scripture is:

> A reverential fear for the LORD; it is exhibited by worship and obedience. The term ... indicates both an attraction to and a shrinking back from the object. The attraction to the LORD is adoration for the majesty and power and glory of the LORD; the shrinking back is the acknowledgment that he is the sovereign judge of all the earth and must be obeyed.[1]

'Only within this framework,' says the psalmist in the style of Wisdom literature, 'is happiness achieved, with all living in harmony and all activities successful and productive.' Such happiness is described with words that evoke memories first of the Garden of Eden where fruitfulness, eating and labour are prominent themes,[2] and

---

[1] Ross, *A Commentary on the Psalms, Volume 3* (90–150), p693.
[2] Genesis 1:28; 2:15.

second of the description given by Moses of the Promised Land. The creation account of Genesis 1 celebrates the fruitfulness of the man and the woman living and working together in God's creation before it was tarnished by sin and rebellion. Moses' address to the Israelites in Deuteronomy 8 holds out the hope of life in a land of abundance, where vines and olives grow and bear fruit.[3]

Work, marriage and children in a household where the Lord is feared are described with a collection of terms that imply an enviable well-being and plenty. The psalmist takes us, again in the style of Wisdom literature, from what history and experience prove to be an unachievable ideal towards a promise. The experience of happiness (v1) will be sealed by the promise of blessing from the Lord Himself (v4) for the one who fears the Lord. Such blessing tells us that Eden can be restored and that we can live with the abundance of the Lord's blessing.

The pilgrims' response (vv4-5)

The possibility of Eden being restored as the Lord pours out His blessing on those who fear Him brings about two sets of responses which could well be seen as the prayers of two pilgrims. The first pilgrim prays for the Lord's blessing from Zion, the place where He was gloriously present in the temple with His people. Paraphrased, his prayer could read, 'May the glory of the Lord shine out of Zion, bringing His radiant light and splendour to all people.' The second pilgrim responds, praying that they would live in the prosperity that comes from Jerusalem: the righteous judgement, security, ordered relationships,

---

[3] Deuteronomy 8:6-10.

well-being and *shalom* already prayed for by these pilgrims in Psalm 122:5-9.

Back to the first pilgrim: he realises another of the consequences of Jerusalem's prosperity and prays that they would see their grandchildren as a result of such blessing. This was not simply for the joy it would bring (and it would!), but because the continuance of the family was an assurance of eternal life. It was the fulfilment of the promise made to Abraham: 'I'm establishing my covenant between me and you, a covenant that includes your descendants, a covenant that goes on and on and on, a covenant that commits me to be your God and the God of your descendants' (Genesis 17:7, *The Message*).

The second pilgrim can only conclude with words that had been prayed before on their journey: 'Peace be upon Israel!'[4] It was a prayer that the Lord would bestow the riches of His blessing on all who feared the Lord, encompassing every conceivable aspect of their lives as individuals and as households.

Jesus and Psalm 128

There is a danger that Psalm 128 (and 127) could be used from the pulpit to lay down ideals for the traditional nuclear family. Used like this, it excludes those who would have loved to build a family unit like this, or those for whom things have gone wrong. Such an interpretation can also leave a trail of guilt.

Wisdom literature, as we have seen, praises those who live the ideal life, but what does it say to anyone who does not come up to that ideal? That is where we turn to the

---

[4] Psalm 125:5; see also Psalm 122.

Lord Jesus and learn from Him who, as Paul states, 'became to us wisdom from God' (1 Corinthians 1:30).

The family life of Jesus was certainly not ideal. Mary, the mother of Jesus, was unmarried when He was conceived, and Joseph was His stepfather, which meant that Jesus in all likelihood lived with the stigma of illegitimacy. He was also homeless.[5]

> His was a life of conflicting authorities, and he faced a crossfire of voices. He experienced opposition from those whom one would expect to be allies: his own family and the people who took religion seriously. Jesus' life is not a pattern for the traditional family; rather, he shows us how to be involved in, and navigate, the messiness of our lives.[6]

Once, arriving at the house where Jesus was teaching, Mary and Jesus' brothers tried to take charge of Him, accusing Him of being mad. Embarrassed by His teaching and actions, they wanted to control Him and put an end to His activities.[7] Realising their demands, Jesus looked around at those surrounding Him and told them that His family consisted of all those who did the will of His Father.[8]

---

[5] Luke 9:57-58.

[6] Cynthia Long Westfall, 'The Family in the Gospels and Acts' in *The Family in the Bible: Exploring Customs, Culture and Context*, eds Richard S Hess and M David Carroll R (Grand Rapids, MI: Baker Academic, 2003 (Kindle version), part 2, chapter 6.

[7] Note also John's comment that his brothers did not believe in Him (John 7:5).

[8] Mark 3:20-21, 31-35.

This redefinition of the family takes on new dimensions as we listen to Jesus conversing with His disciples in John 13–16. Once Judas Iscariot had left the room, Jesus began to talk to the remaining eleven about His approaching departure. He called them 'little children' (John 13:33), a unique term of affection in the Gospels which could be translated as 'dear little children'. Separation, bereavement and grief were approaching, and Jesus spoke very tenderly to those close to Him, as if they were His family.

This intimacy of relationship increased as the evening progressed. Jesus told His disciples that He was no longer going to call them servants, 'because the servant does not know what the master is doing; but I have called you friends, because I have made known to you everything that I have heard from my Father' (John 15:15). 'To be entrusted with a friend's deepest and most intimate thoughts, motivations, intentions and truth – that is a knowledge far beyond a master–servant relationship.'[9] As their relationship with Jesus deepened, He entrusted to them the full revelation of His coming from the Father and the purposes of His Father.

Two further examples recorded by John take this redefinition of the family still further. As Jesus was dying on the cross, He commended John to Mary as her son and Mary to John as his mother.[10] Mary lost her Son and John lost his Master, but they were grafted into a new family

---

[9] David F Ford, *The Gospel of John: A Theological Commentary* (Grand Rapids, MI: Baker Academic, 2021), p300.
[10] John 19:26-27.

unit by the selfless and loving command of Jesus. A new family was coming to birth.

The wonder of this new family was magnified and affirmed when Mary Magdalene met the risen Christ. He told her that she was to go and tell His disciples that He was ascending to His Father and their Father, to His God and their God.[11] Those who had followed and obeyed Him were brothers and sisters of Jesus, members of a new family.[12] The promise of John's introduction was coming to fulfilment through the death and resurrection of Jesus as He gave the right to all who 'believed in his name' to 'become children of God', 'born, not of blood or of the will of the flesh or of the will of man, but of God' (John 1:12-13). A new family, a new people in Christ, had come into being, blessed (as in Psalm 128:4) by the Father beyond all imagining as His sons and daughters in 'his beloved Son' (Colossians 1:13).

The restoration of Eden is no longer just an ideal; it is a reality of our faith in Christ. We have been blessed 'in Christ with every spiritual blessing in the heavenly places' (Ephesians 1:3). By the end of the New Testament, Eden restored is a reality assured in the New Jerusalem, from which we are blessed!

Praying Psalm 128 as a follower of Jesus

If we are going to pray this psalm today, there are three questions we must answer as followers of Jesus:

- What does it mean for us to fear the Lord?

---

[11] John 20:17.
[12] Hebrews 2:17.

- What does the ideal household mean for us?
- How are the blessings of verses 5-6 to be understood?

What does it mean for us as followers of Jesus to 'fear the LORD'?

In the Old Testament, the fear of the Lord is the result of keeping the commandments of the Lord.[13]

But this presents a problem, says Paul, because 'I do not understand my own actions. For I do not do what I want, but I do the very thing I hate' (Romans 7:15). Paul's experience is the experience of us all. How can we ever say that we keep the Lord's commandments and therefore actually fear the Lord?

The problem is solved completely in the Lord Jesus. As we approach the Lord God, we become aware of His all-consuming holiness and utterly ashamed of our own sinfulness and failure. But at our side is One who has taken our filthy garments on Himself and given to us His own righteousness. Now, with sin confessed and forgiven and clothed with the righteousness of Christ, we can draw near with true assurance of faith to the holy and perfect God whenever we need to.

> No condemnation now I dread;
> Jesus, and all in Him, is mine!
> Alive in Him, my living Head,
> And clothed in righteousness Divine,
> Bold I approach the eternal throne,
> And claim the crown through Christ my own.[14]

---

[13] Deuteronomy 6:1-2.

[14] From the hymn 'And can it be' by Charles Wesley (1707–88).

To fear the Lord for the followers of the Lord Jesus means that we can 'approach the throne of grace with boldness, so that we may receive mercy and find grace to help in time of need' (Hebrews 4:16). We fear the Lord, we worship Him in His glory and majesty, and we stand forgiven and righteous before His throne of judgement, only because of the Lord Jesus who ushers us into His Father's presence and assures us of our eternal standing before Him as His dear children.

What does the ideal household in Psalm 128 mean for us as followers of Jesus?

The household in the Old Testament was one where the stranger was to be welcomed and cared for as a guest, and could include immigrants seeking refuge, the weak, the elderly, servants, the fatherless and widows. All these were to be valued, cared for and respected. The Old Testament household was a home that included and welcomed a wide variety of people, as the story of Ruth makes clear.

Equally, the New Testament picture of the family goes well beyond our Western concepts of the nuclear family. Just as John took Mary into his own home as commanded by Jesus, there were always those outside the immediate family who must be cared for. The community of Christians that came into being after the descent of the Holy Spirit at Pentecost was one in which love and care for their fellow-Christians superseded natural family relationships. Later, we read that 'the whole group of those who believed were of one heart and soul, and no one claimed private ownership of any possessions, but everything they owned was held in common' (Acts 4:32).

It is the Spirit of Christ, who lives within us and moves among us to form us into the image of Christ, who teaches us to live with this welcoming and sacrificial generosity.

Other examples in the New Testament which go beyond the limits of the nuclear family are found in the epistles. Paul welcomed the runaway slave Onesimus as his own son and encouraged Philemon to take him back as a brother in Christ. Timothy was like a son to Paul. Mark was like a son to Peter. The members of John's churches and Paul's churches in Galatia were their 'little children' (1 John 2:1).[15]

The New Testament contains comprehensive instructions for the family life of parents and children,[16] but it also teaches us to reach beyond our immediate family relationships and, compelled by the Spirit of Christ, draw into our extended communities those in need of support, hospitality and friendship. Biblical family life is to extend well beyond the boundaries of our blood relationships.[17]

How are the blessings of verses 5-6 to be understood?

Blessing bestowed by the Lord is described twice in this psalm. The first is in verse 4. Fearing the Lord will bring His blessing. But, our responses to instructions to fear the Lord and keep His commandments[18] are like New Year's resolutions: temporary and always prone to failure.

---

[15] See Philemon 1; Philippians 2:22; 1 Peter 5:13; Galatians 4:19.

[16] See, for example, Ephesians 5:22-6:4.

[17] See, for example, Romans 12:13; Hebrews 13:2.

[18] Deuteronomy 31:19-21.

The blessings of verses 5 and 6 were secured at the cross where our failures were paid for; they were eternally assured by Christ's resurrection and ascension: a Man in heaven for us, seated at the right hand of the Father, who pours His blessings on us because of Jesus. We experience the Father's blessing in our daily lives as we live hidden in Christ and united to Him. Glorious as this is, there is more to say!

These blessings the Father has bestowed on us in Christ are infinitely more than a day-by-day experience. They have eternal implications. The second reference to the blessings bestowed by the Lord in verses 5 and 6 speaks of these coming from Zion and Jerusalem, the earthly goal of every pilgrim. The New Testament wonderfully enriches these pictures and places them in the entirely new dimension of eternity!

> You have not come to something that can be touched, a blazing fire, and darkness, and gloom, and a tempest, and the sound of a trumpet, and a voice whose words made the hearers beg that not another word be spoken to them. (For they could not endure the order that was given, 'If even an animal touches the mountain, it shall be stoned to death.' Indeed, so terrifying was the sight that Moses said, 'I tremble with fear.') But you have come to Mount Zion and to the city of the living God, the heavenly Jerusalem, and to innumerable angels in festal gathering, and to the assembly of the firstborn who are enrolled in heaven, and to God the judge of all, and to the spirits of the righteous made perfect, and to Jesus, the mediator of a new

covenant, and to the sprinkled blood that speaks a better word than the blood of Abel.
(Hebrews 12:18-24)

Arriving at the new Mount Zion, there is no shrinking back or trembling, no dark cloud or thunder and no trumpets to warn us against stepping onto holy ground. There is no voice that thunders, causing us to fear.[19] The blessing is one of welcome, joy and glorious reunions with all those who have been brought finally to this indefinably safe and assured place through Christ. The psalmist's prayer of verse 5a has been answered.

But he goes further, praying that we might 'see the prosperity of Jerusalem' (verse 5b). Unimaginable wealth and riches are in the New Jerusalem described by John:

And in the spirit he carried me away to a great, high mountain and showed me the holy city Jerusalem coming down out of heaven from God. It has the glory of God and a radiance like a very rare jewel, like jasper, clear as crystal.
(Revelation 21:10-11)

Arriving in the New Jerusalem, we shall be in the very presence of God, seeing His glory and radiance, blessed in Christ beyond anything we could possibly deserve or expect. Sin, failure, tears, struggle and death are completely forgotten as we wonder at the beauty, the holiness and the love of the Father who welcomes us in His Son, Jesus Christ, standing with arms outstretched to embrace His returning prodigal children.

---

[19] See Exodus 19.

Responding

We have seen that the fear of the Lord means confessing Him as the sovereign judge of all the earth, who must be obeyed, as well as adoring Him for His majesty, power and glory. Do your prayers reflect this penitence and this adoration?

How does this psalm challenge you to pray and work towards church fellowships that become communities extending well beyond the boundaries of the nuclear family?

Does the prayer of the two pilgrims in verses 5 and 6 encourage you to pray similarly for the Lord's blessing? How might their example change the way you pray?

10
Psalm 129
Oppressed and Wounded

¹ 'Often have they attacked me from my youth'
– let Israel now say –
² 'often have they attacked me from my youth,
yet they have not prevailed against me.
³ Those who plough ploughed on my back;
they made their furrows long.'
⁴ The LORD is righteous;
he has cut the cords of the wicked.
⁵ May all who hate Zion
be put to shame and turned back.
⁶ Let them be like the grass on the housetops
that withers before it grows up,
⁷ with which reapers do not fill their hands
or binders of sheaves their arms,
⁸ while those who pass by do not say,
'The blessing of the LORD be upon you!
We bless you in the name of the LORD!'

Introducing Psalm 129

We come to the third of the Psalms of Ascents which deals with suffering. Rather than the suffering caused by contempt and ridicule, or by events that threaten us, the psalmist writes here of the extreme pain of physical suffering felt by the afflicted. Cruel actions have left the narrator oppressed, bound by tight ropes and sorely wounded.

Some commentators have expressed surprise that this psalm should be included in the Psalms of Ascents, but suffering was woven into every part of Israel's history, and these pilgrims were not afraid to recount the toughest parts of their story and their experiences as they journeyed to Jerusalem. They would have reminded themselves of Israel's history: a long narrative of suffering in which chapter after chapter told the same harrowing story. Again and again, says the psalmist, Israel has been like someone who from childhood has lain bound on the earth as a farmer ploughs long furrows down his back (v3).

The same image was used by the prophets. Isaiah foretold a day when his nation's tormentors would walk over their prostrate captives, and Micah, prophesying in the time of Jeremiah, spoke of a time to come when the city of Zion would be ploughed like a field.[1] But here in Psalm 129, the suffering is personified with an immediacy that is even more horrifying and dreadful. Israel, the child loved by God and called by Him out of Egypt,[2] has been bound and tortured from those early years. The repetition in verse 2 suggests that suffering has only increased as time has passed. Through it all, however, Israel's enduring trust in the Lord's righteousness and His protection has meant that their enemies have never finally overcome them.

---

[1] Isaiah 51:23; Jeremiah 26:18.
[2] Exodus 4:22-23; Hosea 11:1.

Could Israel, the Lord's child, tolerate such suffering? Yes! The second half of verse 2 suggests that it has been borne with a stubbornness that would not even accept the possibility of defeat. The psalmist arrives at verse 4 with a confident statement of belief that overrides all the hardships experienced by Israel: 'The LORD is righteous'! The Lord, Israel's covenant-keeping, promise-keeping Lord by His nature is just and saving. As the Lord declared through Isaiah, 'There is no other god besides me, a righteous God and a Saviour; there is no one besides me' (Isaiah 45:21). Israel's God will not allow His beloved son to remain wounded and dying in a ploughed field. The ropes that have bound Israel are cut and he is set free. Israel discovers once again that the Lord saves and delivers.

An oppressed and cruelly wounded Israel has been rescued, but the psalmist continues in verses 5 to 8 with words that are hard to comprehend. He prays for the dishonouring and departure of all those who hate Zion.[3] He asks that they become like the meagre grass on sun-baked roofs which withers and never produces a harvest. The image shifts slightly as the one praying asks that those who hate Israel become like those who carry home a failed harvest, never to receive a blessing from those that pass by. The reference is to the story of Ruth and the greeting of Boaz to reapers returning from the fields with the beautiful words, 'The LORD be with you!' The reapers then

---

[3] Zion can be understood as referring to the city of Jerusalem and/or to the Lord's people.

replied, 'The LORD bless you.'[4] For the enemies of Zion there is only a profound silence.

Is it right for the psalmist who worships a holy, loving God to pray like this? Does not Israel worship a Lord whose purposes are those of steadfast love and mercy? If we can understand that the psalmist, along with all of suffering humanity, is expressing a passionate longing for justice and for the vindication of those who suffer unjustly, then we are beginning to find an answer to this question. The cry of verses 5 to 8 reveals the sheer depths of hurt and pain in the human heart. To suggest that people do not have the right to cry out to God in this way when their suffering takes them to breaking point is to imply that God does not understand the pain of the human predicament.[5] That suggestion is completely contradicted by the suffering of the Servant recounted in Isaiah 53 and the New Testament message of the Messiah who in Himself bears the grievous totality of the sin, pain and judgement of all people.

There is another aspect to the prayer of these verses. Israel, God's chosen people, was called to display the glory of God to all nations so that they too would be blessed.[6] If, however, Israel's oppression and wounding were fatal, the purposes of God would be frustrated and His glory would remain hidden. That is why the psalmist

---

[4] Ruth 2:4.

[5] The psalmist is not alone as he prays like this. King David, fleeing for his life from his subversive son Absalom prays in Psalm 3 that his enemies might be struck on the cheek and their teeth broken. Other psalmists pray for the destruction of their enemies. The harshest cries for vengeance are found in Psalm 109 and 137:7-9.

[6] Isaiah 60:1-3; Genesis 12:1-3.

hated those who hated Zion. 'Destroy Zion,' he says, 'and you destroy the people of the Lord and the place where His glory is displayed to the world by His presence in the temple.'

Jesus and Psalm 129

As we have seen, Jesus was the One in whom the destiny of the nation chosen by God would come to its fulfilment. It happened as the Son of God took upon Himself human flesh and blood. Living a life of perfect obedience and submission to His Father, fulfilling all the demands of the law, He faced the most pervasive testing by Satan, as well as rejection and unbelief from those He came to save. Through all this, the Son of God learned obedience:

> Jesus, as a human being, suffered and was limited and was weak, but his pain taught him obedience, not faithless despair ...; his frailty deepened his reverence for God rather than stiffening his rebellion ... Pressed into the muck and mire of human anguish, Jesus never forgot that he was the Son.[7]

The oppression that Jesus suffered was indeed the 'muck and mire of human anguish'. He experienced the indescribable shame of being bound on His arrest. His back was ploughed by the whips and lashes of Roman soldiers. Led out to crucifixion, He suffered what was probably the cruellest form of execution ever devised. Physical suffering was multiplied immeasurably as Jesus

---

[7] Long, *Hebrews*, p68.

carried within Himself and on Himself the entire weight of the world's sin; the world went totally dark for three hours. The deep infection of sin that ruined us all was confronted by the sinlessness of the One who did no wrong. Bound, deeply wounded and weighed down by the burden of the world's sin and suffering, He bore the judgement of a righteous God, as He was made sin for us.

The cross is in itself the final answer to the prayer of verse 5 to 8 because it is there that God's judgement on sin is met by His incalculable mercy and forgiveness. The righteousness and steadfast love of God met there and, three days later, the whole course of the history of the universe was changed as the purposes of God prevailed. His Son could not be bound in death. God 'raised him from the dead and seated him at his right hand in the heavenly places' (Ephesians 1:20).

By His death and resurrection and by the glory of His ascension and exaltation, Jesus turned the negativity and condemnation of the last four verses of this difficult psalm into forgiveness and blessing. This is grace: sheer, extravagant grace, totally undeserved and wonderfully surprising!

Reading Psalm 129 as a follower of Jesus

Once we set out on our journey with Christ, Scripture repeatedly warns us to expect nothing less than daily temptations and the constant attacks of the evil one. Living united to Jesus Christ, we are prey to the constant temptation of 'wanting to be untrue to God …

freeing ourselves from God ... living constantly in doubt of God'.[8]

A young man who had only just become a Christian told me that, having given his life to Jesus Christ, he was constantly besieged by doubts about the truth of what had happened to him. Talking it through at length did little to dispel those doubts. So we turned to the Bible, to words written by Peter, who knew just what it was like to be tempted: 'Discipline yourselves; keep alert. Like a roaring lion your adversary the devil prowls around, looking for someone to devour. Resist him, steadfast in your faith, for you know that your brothers and sisters throughout the world are undergoing the same kinds of suffering' (1 Peter 5:8-9).[9] Those words spoke powerfully to him. He looked up at me, saying, 'I'm all right now! I know that I belong to Jesus and that I'm safe!' From the early days of living for Christ to the days of mature discipleship, the attacks of our enemy never lessen. If anything, they increase! His suggestive nagging and persuasive wiles can cause the most alert child of God to stumble, bringing pain and guilt and shame.

As Job found, the testing of our faith is far from straightforward. Like they did for him, questions and doubts can take us down many a cul-de-sac. The theme of the suffering of those who seek to live a righteous life as opposed to the apparent invulnerability of those who deny God and live only for themselves is repeated

---

[8] Helmut Thielicke, *Between God and Satan: The Temptation of Jesus and the Temptability of Man* (Farmington Hills, MI: Oil Lamp Books LLC, 2010), p14.

[9] Peter was speaking from his own experience here. See Matthew 16:21-23; Luke 22:31-34.

throughout the Bible. Faithful endurance at such times of suffering is the result of faith schooled in the classroom of the nature, character and acts of the Lord. He is our faithful, promise-keeping, steadfastly loving Lord who has acted to reconcile us to Himself through Jesus Christ and who strengthens us by His Holy Spirit when we suffer.

I will never forget visiting a friend who was seriously ill in hospital. After talking and praying together, I was about to leave. She grasped my hand and said, 'D'you know, I wouldn't have missed all this for anything. I have never known the love of God and of His people like this before.' We may not understand His purposes, but as we endure, we can discover that they are to be trusted.

Allen Gardiner, the founder of the South American Mission Society, knew that he was called by God to reach Indian tribes in South America that had not been reached by other missions. In 1838, he crossed the Andes Mountains on a mule. His only aim was to tell unreached tribes the good news of Jesus Christ. Every attempt to reach the Indians failed. Then, in the early 1850s, he sailed south with six other men in an attempt to reach the tribes in southern Argentina. Tragically shipwrecked on the treacherous coast of Tierra del Fuego, their bodies were found by a search party, hidden underneath the boat in which they had taken refuge during their last days. Surviving until their remaining provisions ran out, death came slowly to each of them. Allen Gardiner's journal records his final entry: 'What continued mercies am I receiving at the hands of my heavenly Father! Blessed be His holy name! ... Great and marvellous are the loving-

144

kindnesses of my gracious God unto me.'[10] In his afflictions he had discovered the Lord's rescuing love and he could proclaim with the psalmist, 'The LORD is righteous' (v4).

As Christians, we live in a minority surrounded by those who mock or dismiss our faith. Can we actually pray with the psalmist that those who actively oppose us will be brought to shame? The Christian's prayer is different. It is modelled on the prayer of Jesus, who prayed for His tormentors and for those who crucified Him, 'Father, forgive them; for they do not know what they are doing.' (Luke 23:34). There was no plea for vindication. His prayer was that those who afflicted Him would confess that the crucified One hanging before them was indeed the Son of God. That prayer was certainly answered when the Roman centurion confessed this in front of his platoon of soldiers.

Responding

An experienced mountaineer carries equipment for every condition that the mountain might throw at them. What 'equipment' do you think we need in order to face the suffering and storms that life throws at us? See 1 Peter 5:6-10.

It is helpful sometimes to write your own psalm expressing the pain and hurts you have suffered. When the psalmists wrote like this, there was nearly always a renewal of trust in their Lord by the time they had finished (eg Psalm 13).

---

[10] John Marsh and Waite Stirling, *The Story of Commander Allen Gardiner* (London, James Nisbet & Co, 1877), p81.

11
Psalm 130
Crying From the Depths

¹ Out of the depths I cry to you, O LORD.
Lord, hear my voice!
Let your ears be attentive
to the voice of my supplications!
³ If you, O LORD, should mark iniquities,
Lord, who could stand?
⁴ But there is forgiveness with you,
so that you may be revered.
⁵ I wait for the LORD, my soul waits,
and in his word I hope;
⁶ my soul waits for the Lord
more than those who watch for the morning,
more than those who watch for the morning.
⁷ O Israel, hope in the LORD!
For with the LORD there is steadfast love,
and with him is great power to redeem.
⁸ It is he who will redeem Israel
from all its iniquities.

Introducing Psalm 130

Psalm 130 is the prayer of a pilgrim overwhelmed by trouble crying out to the Lord.

His deep despair is expressed in the first two verses of the psalm with utter frankness. The succeeding three pairs of verses climb a staircase from the depths as the psalmist's willingness to be real and honest before God is answered by a steadily growing assurance of hope.

'The depths' are often used in the Psalms as a metaphor for distress, a picture of a person drowning in a sea of troubles. The source of these troubles varies from betrayal by friends (Psalm 69), attack from enemies (Psalm 124), to an overwhelming sense of being deserted or punished by God (Psalm 42; 88).

The despair in Psalm 130 is tangible and deeply disturbing, but how much worse it would have been if there was no one to whom the cry could be directed. 'Out of the depths I cry' must be the most poignant cry of the human heart, and without anyone to hear or listen, those depths will be the bleakest and loneliest place. This psalmist, however, has previously experienced that the Lord of steadfast love is present even in the worst of circumstances. We have no idea what overwhelming troubles this pilgrim had experienced, but his cry of despair was a cry directed specifically to the Lord, the God of covenant, steadfast love. It seemed that his previous experiences had taught him that the Lord would hear his cry from the chasm of darkness.[1] Shafts of light pierced the darkness of despair as the psalmist's cry for rescue was heard and he discovered that the Lord would come to him carrying four gifts which combined to bring hope where before there was no hope.

---

[1] See Psalm 139:7-8.

The first gift bringing light into the psalmist's darkness is the discovery that the Lord is present with forgiveness (vv3-4). He has revealed Himself to His people as a God who is merciful, loving and forgiving, and when He acts with forgiveness, He refuses to remember our offences. If He were a God who kept a record of our wrongs, human existence would be intolerable and even impossible. The Lord to whom the psalmist cries out reminds him that He is utterly determined to forgive. He will go to the greatest lengths to forgive those who want to serve Him with reverence and fear:

> The heart of this psalm is in its simple statement of dogma. It is not a prayer for forgiveness. It is a statement that forgiveness is there, and available. That is all. There is no speculation, and no subjective yearning about it … It is plain statement. Here am I, and there is God, and God will act.[2]

The Lord has heard the cry from the depths, and the realisation dawns on the psalmist that forgiveness is a gift that his Lord longs to give.

Then comes the second gift, that of patient waiting with endurance (v5). The word used for 'wait' in this verse is derived from a word that means to twist or stretch a many-stranded rope to near breaking point. The one praying is stretched to the limit, longing for an answer. The first gift of promised forgiveness has reminded him that the Lord is always true to His Word. Now he knows that the wait,

---

[2] Eric Routley, *Ascent to the Cross: Meditations on the Pilgrimage Psalms* (Nashville, TN: Abingdon Press, 1962), p57.

long though it may be, will be worth it because it is a wait with hope.

Two gifts have been given. But before the final two are given, the theme of waiting grasps the psalmist's imagination. He digresses to paint a vivid picture (vv6-7a) of a night watchman standing guard on the city walls. Long, lonely waiting in the cold, dark hours of the night is rewarded as the first glimmer of light appears in the east, heralding the dawn of sunrise. The watchman knows for sure that the sun will rise above the horizon and that the whole scene before him will soon be flooded with its light and warmth. The psalmist's picture tells him that the seemingly interminable tension of waiting will end as certainly as the sun rises in the morning. His waiting can be endured because there is the assurance that it is only for a season. The Lord will come, and when He does, He brings two final gifts to encourage and restore (v7b).

The third gift is a new understanding and experience of the Lord's 'steadfast love'. The Hebrew word for 'love' here is *hesed*, one of the great words of the Old Testament. This steadfast love is the assured loving-kindness of the Lord, unchanging and freely given to those who do not deserve or even ask for it.

Hard on its heels comes the fourth gift of full redemption described with two different words. 'Redeem' in verse 7 means a full and complete cutting free from all that spoils and darkens life. 'Redeem' in verse 8 means an intervention by the Lord to ransom His people from everything that holds them hostage. Taking the two verses together, the final gift, given without limit, is the Lord's comprehensive rescue from the depths, the final answer to the psalmist's cry of despair in verse 1.

Four gifts have been brought by the Lord. Forgiveness, which always accompanies the Lord, is followed by patient endurance given to wait in hope for Him to act on the promise of His Word. Close behind those two gifts, the Lord brings His covenant love and His redemption. Rescued, the psalmist begins to discover that he is secure. The cry of the heart from the depths has been heard and answered. Hope has been restored!

Jesus and Psalm 130

We stand on holy ground as we consider Jesus and this psalm. Taking this psalm on His lips, He would not have been praying for Himself but for all people whose lives are ruined by sin, with all its despair and ghastly consequences. 'He took the place of many sinners and prayed that they might be forgiven' (Isaiah 53:12, GNT), passing through depths far deeper than the psalmist had ever known as He cried out in utter dereliction from the cross, 'My God, my God, why have you forsaken me?' (Mark 15:34).

Jesus knew that He was to be crucified on a cross and that His dead body would be laid in a tomb. Satan's rule of sin and death over men and women could only be broken in a conflict which we can never begin to comprehend. Only by the descent of the Lord Jesus into the profoundest depths beyond all human experience to do battle with sin, its accompanying judgement and with death itself could atonement for sin be achieved. The result of that battle was triumphantly declared by His resurrection to new life on the third day.

Raised victoriously from His profound experience of the depths, Jesus comes to us bearing the gifts that the psalmist writes about. He can bring us forgiveness because all the sin and guilt of failed humanity was concentrated onto Him in the three hours of darkness preceding his death. Battle raged and spiritual forces warred as never before. The judgement of the righteous Father was meted out to His blameless Son on behalf of all people. Jesus accepted that judgement with the inevitability of banishment into the depths of darkness far away from His Father's presence. Satan roared as he tried in vain to grasp and hold on to the One whose steps he had shadowed for nearly thirty years. Not only did his attempts to hold the Rescuer fail, but he was also totally defeated. Atonement was made for sin and every effect of sin so that the gift of forgiveness could now be received from the nail-scarred hands of the risen Saviour.

The risen Christ comes to us as One who entered and endured the depths of suffering with complete trust in His Father. He endured the assaults of the evil one throughout His life as He waited patiently for His hour to come. He waited patiently in suffering and death with complete faith in His Father. His endurance and trust in all that He suffered in life and death was for us, so that we would not grow weary in waiting and lose heart when we cry out from the depths.[3]

As well as His gifts of forgiveness and patient endurance in waiting, His cry from the depths was a cry that the Lord would honour His pre-creation covenant of unfailing, steadfast love set upon men and women. Every

---

[3] Hebrews 4:15-16; 12:2-3.

scriptural covenant is ratified by a sacrifice, and by His sacrificial death, the Lord Jesus sealed the promise of love declared by His Father. As Christ died for sin, His Father's free gift of pledged love was poured out for all who would receive it.

The final gift as Jesus cried out from the depths for men and women was that of abundant redemption. The same idea is used to describe the ransom of the firstborn from death on the night of the first Passover in Egypt.[4] The price paid for that ransom was a sacrificed lamb, redeeming those who sheltered under its shed blood from the fate of the Egyptian firstborn. The idea of ransom in the Old Testament is also associated with the idea of the kinsman redeemer, a relative who intervened to release a family member sold into slavery. As He went to the depths, Jesus became for us the Passover lamb, releasing from slavery all who shelter under His shed blood. Being unashamed to call Himself our brother,[5] He gave Himself as our kinsman redeemer, intervening to redeem us from the slavery of sin.

Forgiveness, patient endurance, steadfast love and abundant redemption: four gifts brought to us by Christ, our praying Saviour, who descended to the depths on our behalf.

Praying Psalm 130 as a follower of Jesus

Here is waiting prayer from the depths filled with tension and pain, but now we know it is prayer that has been

---

[4] Exodus 12.
[5] Hebrews 2:11.

prayed on our behalf by the Lord Jesus in His suffering and affliction.

A close friend suffered a deep depression in his early professional years as a college lecturer. Sinking to the depths, he spent days in isolation, refusing any help and company as he lay on his bed with his face towards the wall. Anger with God welled up continually, which he once tried to abate by ripping his Bible into shreds. But it was all to no avail – for one reason. Whatever happened and whatever he tried, he could not escape from the presence of the Lord who was with him and who would never leave him. Healing came only slowly, but it came, and with it the accompanying promise of God's blessing.

The Hebrew word for 'depths' in verse 1 expresses the deepest pain and anguish, but it is usually coupled wonderfully in the Old Testament with the promise of the Lord's deliverance. Isaiah 51:9-11 describes the rescue of the Lord's redeemed people from the Egyptian armies as the waters of the Red Sea were dried up when the 'great deep' actually became an escape route for them. David's despair as he was sinking into the depths without any foothold in Psalm 69 was answered as he joined with heaven, earth and the seas in praise. Jesus demonstrated in His authority over creation, evil powers, illness and suffering that anything that threatens to destroy us is under His sovereign control. The rescue prayed for in Psalm 130 is finally assured because of the complete effectiveness of Christ's atoning work on the cross and His victory over death. On the cross He mediated between a sinful world and His Father and sealed that mediation for ever by His resurrection, ascension and exaltation.

Only a Mediator who descended into the hell of human rebellion against God can conclude our long war with the Father. Only a Christ who willingly received the lethal consequences of our sin can truly take away the burden of them. Only one who has been there, in the hell of our making, can comfort us in our suffering. If Jesus didn't get all the way to the bottom of our predicament, our lost and forsaken condition, then we are left unredeemed at the root. We will be forever lonely, ever tarred with shame, never feeling known, never at peace. But because Jesus entered fully into the deathliness of our human existence, then he can bring us into the eternal life of the Triune God.[6]

When we are sinking to the depths, we come to Jesus Christ only to discover that He was there before we were. Because He took upon Himself our humanity, 'even death on a cross' (Philippians 2:8), He ministers to us in the darkest depths, where He suffered all the results of the reign of sin: guilt, depression, grief, loneliness, hopelessness, betrayal and the most agonising pain. Bearing that load on the cross and in death, He overcame its root cause, finally defeating Satan and his legions. Sin and every consequence of sin was erased for the Christian so that no record exists of that which ruined and overwhelmed us. We would be mired in the depths if God kept a record of our wrongs, but in Christ that is not so. With Him there is the wonderful gift of forgiveness.

---

[6] Gerrit Dawson, *Raising Adam: Why Jesus Descended into Hell* (Edinburgh: Handsel Press, 2018), Introduction (Kindle version).

Alongside that gift are given two more: those of steadfast love and redemption. The essential nature of love is the complete giving of oneself. God demonstrated the depths of His love for us in not sparing His own Son but giving Him up for us all (Romans 8:32). As Paul goes on to say, the love of God demonstrated in Jesus Christ is something from which we can never be separated. So we are not dismayed by troubles, hard times, hatred, hunger, homelessness, threats or wounds. The fact is that:

> nothing living or dead, angelic or demonic, today or tomorrow, high or low, thinkable or unthinkable – absolutely *nothing* can get between us and God's love because of the way that Jesus our Master has embraced us.
> (Romans 8:38-39, *The Message*)

The rescue plan of the Father, worked out by Jesus Christ, is complete, for 'with the LORD there is steadfast love, and with him is great power to redeem' (v7).

Those are the facts of our redemption, but for now anguish may often be an inescapable reality on our journey. When life becomes a pain-soaked and never-ending struggle, words with which to pray may well fail us. The wordless cry from the depths may be all we can summon as we wait for God to answer and rescue. This is when we need the gift of patient endurance. Our agonised cry is taken up in the infinite wisdom and comprehension of the indwelling Holy Spirit. He helps us in our weakness, interceding with sighs too deep for words as the Lord grants to us His gift of patient, trusting endurance. Can our waiting then be borne?

Simeon, described by Luke as a 'righteous and devout' man,[7] had waited for long years, and his wait must have seemed interminable. For most of his life, he had lived through the cruel Roman occupation and the ruthless tyranny of Herod and his family. Earlier in Simeon's life, the Roman general, Pompey, had waged war on Jerusalem for three long months, killing thousands of Jews. Experiencing those traumatic events and the intensity of that suffering, he would have almost certainly prayed, 'Out of the depths I cry to you, O LORD!' Was it during that dark time that God had promised that he would meet his longed-for Messiah? Faithful Simeon had waited and waited, stretched nearly to breaking point, enduring patiently and praying for thirty years for the fulfilment of the Lord's promise that before he died he would actually meet Israel's Messiah.

Then one day, the Holy Spirit prompted him to go into the temple courts. As he obeyed, his waiting ended and his prayers were fulfilled. He met Joseph and Mary with their newborn child. Taking the baby in his arms, he knew that he was holding the infant Messiah, and he broke into praise, worshipping God and saying:

> Master, now you are dismissing your servant in peace,
> according to your word;
> For my eyes have seen your salvation,
> which you have prepared in the presence of all peoples,
> a light for revelation to the Gentiles

---

[7] Luke 2:25.

and for glory to your people Israel.
(Luke 2:29-32)

The tension of waiting stretching through all those years had ended. The night watch ended and the light dawned as Simeon came face to face with the Messiah and held Him close in his arms.

When the waiting is at its hardest, and the night watch seems endless, the psalmist affirms that dawn is promised. Darkness will end and light will come. The patient waiting with the gift of endurance will come to an end because of Jesus Christ, the 'morning star' (Revelation 22:16), rising with hope at the end of every night watch. He comes with unfailing love and full redemption and He will redeem the Lord's people from every sin and all suffering.

Responding

The Lord comes to us in this psalm with four gifts: forgiveness, patient endurance, steadfast love and redemption. How real are these gifts to you?

Can you remind yourself of a time when a new assurance of faith dawned after a night of doubting?

Are you waiting and waiting for an answer to a prayer that you have been praying for years? The prophet Micah was determined to wait as well as to trust confidently that the Lord would answer: 'As for me, I will look to the LORD; I will wait for the God of my salvation; my God will hear me' (Micah 7:7). Let Micah and this psalm encourage you to wait patiently for the Lord to answer.

12
Psalm 131
Learning to Trust

¹ O LORD, my heart is not lifted up,
my eyes are not raised too high;
I do not occupy myself with things
too great and too marvellous for me.
² But I have calmed and quieted my soul,
like a weaned child with its mother;
my soul is like the weaned child that is with me.
³ O Israel, hope in the LORD
from this time on and for evermore.

Introducing Psalm 131

The Lord takes His rightful place (v1a)

Rescued from the depths, the psalmist in Psalm 130 discovered a new security as the Lord came to him bringing gifts of forgiveness, endurance, love and redemption. As a result, at the outset of Psalm 131, things are different.

Nothing is allowed to come before the name of the Lord at the very beginning. Psalm 130 started with the psalmist's cry of distress. Now he cannot wait to speak the covenant name of his Lord. It is a wonderful confession of trust! As we have seen before, the name 'LORD' (in capitals) in most English translations replaces the personal name of God.[1] YHWH (usually transliterated as Yahweh) was the name by which God revealed Himself to the people of Israel through Moses: 'I AM WHO I AM' (Exodus 3:14). The psalmist is reminding himself and all who are listening that his God is Yahweh, the God who always is, who is eternally present with His people, and who will be constantly faithful as God to His people. The psalmist was formerly crying from the depths; now he has discovered a renewed confidence in his Lord as the God of steadfast love, mercy and salvation.

The psalmist acknowledges the majesty and wonder of the Lord (v1a)

Declaring the Lord's name, he realises the sheer majesty and holiness of the One he is addressing. Pride and ambition are impossible in the presence of the Lord:

> It is almost impossible to be lofty and high without becoming people who see themselves as impressive and important, as godlets. The difference between God and us is that God never thinks he is us ... A lofty heart and high eyes lead to action that treats me as the only person that counts.[2]

After all his suffering, the psalmist comes to the same conclusion as Job: ' See, I am of small account; what shall

---

[1] This originates from Jewish practice. The personal name of God was viewed as so holy that it should never be spoken aloud. Instead of reading the word YHWH, they replaced it with the Hebrew word *adonay*, meaning Lord. (See the introduction to most modern Bible translations. For example: NIV, NRSV, ESV.)

[2] Goldingay, *Psalms: Volume 3: Psalms 90–150*, pp535-536.

I answer you?' (Job 40:4). The Lord's greatness, authority, power, righteousness, eternity and absolute justice lead the psalmist to the place where pride is abandoned and the heart is bowed. He is in the presence of the holy Lord and his eyes are lowered lest he see the glory and holiness of the Lord and be consumed.[3]

The psalmist's questioning comes to an end (v1b)

In the bleakness of the previous psalm, questions could well have engulfed the psalmist. 'Why did God allow this to happen? Can He really be who He says He is?' But as the Lord's love and redemption dawn, he makes the conscious decision that such questioning cannot be allowed to rule his life. 'I cannot continue to interrogate the Lord. I am not privy to His counsels. He knows the beginning from the end and I certainly do not. I hardly know myself, but He knows me and I am settled now on a path of trusting in His ways and plans for me. He is higher and wiser than any human understanding and I have decided to trust Him, come what may!'

The final decision (v2)[4]

The psalmist's stubborn and argumentative will has now been quietened. The turmoil has gone and he is at peace. He has decided to level and compose himself like a contented child in its mother's arms, at ease and calm. His

---

[3] Exodus 33:12-23; Isaiah 6:1-5; Ezekiel 1.

[4] Kidner comments on the problem of translating verse 2 as follows: 'The RV translates it most faithfully: "Like a weaned child with his mother, My soul is with me like a weaned child."' Derek Kidner, *Psalms 73–150*, p448

sights are not set on anything that is proud or beyond his reach. One commentator writes:

> I believe we must translate Psalm 131:2 as follows: 'But on the contrary, I have made myself without resistance or movement ... just as one does with his mother, thus have I made myself content.'[5]

Accepting that he will never fully understand the ways of the Lord, he has decided to trust in his Lord and in the security of His promises.

A public declaration of faith (v3)

Finally, the psalmist insists on standing before the Lord's people to tell them what has transpired between him and his Lord. 'See how He has dealt with me and where I am standing now, people of God,' he declares. 'Here is the Lord! You can hope in Him with complete trust, now and always!'

Jesus and Psalm 131

Jesus prays to His Father (v1)

The long sessions of prayer in Gethsemane were times of deep anguish for Jesus. Crucifixion lay ahead, which would bring indescribable suffering and the dread of separation from His Father. 'Jesus came to be with the

---

[5] P. A. H.de Boer, Psalm cxxxi 2, Vetus Testamentum 16, 1966, pp291-292.

Father for an interlude before his betrayal, but found hell rather than heaven opened before him and he staggered.'[6]

The psalmist came to his Lord with a heart not lifted up and eyes not raised too high. Only Jesus, the perfect, sinless Son of God, could stand in the presence of His Father, but knowing that He would carry the unbearable weight of the sin of the world, He fell to the ground and, kneeling, prayed, 'Father, if you are willing, remove this cup from me; yet, not my will but yours be done' (Luke 22:42).[7]

Every minute of the hours that Jesus spent in prayer was centred on His Father from whom He had come and to whom He would return. The psalmist found a safe place after the storm in the covenant name of His Lord. Facing the storm ahead, Jesus found refuge with His Father. The relationship between the Father and the Son was an eternal relationship of intimate communion, trustful dependence and unity of purpose. Mark 14:36 tells us that when He prayed in Gethsemane, Jesus called God 'Abba', expressing His perfect trust in the will of His Father. Jesus alone, as the Son of the Father, had an intimate knowledge of the Father's will and saving love, and it was to Him alone that the Father had entrusted the outworking of their mutually shared purpose of salvation.[8] So, when facing the judgement of God for the sin and guilt of the world that would shortly be heaped on Him, Jesus was

---

[6] William Lane, *The Gospel of Mark (New International Commentary on the New Testament)* (Grand Rapids, MI: William B Eerdmans Publishing Company, 1974), p516.

[7] It was Jewish practice to stand to pray. But see Mark14:35; Luke 22:41.

[8] Matthew 11:27.

able to come to a place of acceptance because He was accepting it from His Father.

Accepting the Father's will (v2)

We stand on holy ground as we listen to Jesus in Gethsemane: '"I am deeply grieved, even to death; remain here, and keep awake." And going a little farther, he threw himself on the ground and prayed that, if it were possible, the hour might pass from him' (Mark 14:34-35).

Mark's account of Jesus' words and physical symptoms only begins to portray something of the intensity of the dereliction that lay ahead of Him. Jesus told His disciples that His sorrow was such that He was close to death. Luke tells us that as He prayed, His sweat became like large drops of blood falling to the ground, a condition that only occurs when anguish is piled on anguish in the deepest suffering and distress; the capillaries under the skin dilate and bleed through the sweat glands.[9]

Then followed words that changed the destiny of the world: 'Abba, Father, for you all things are possible; remove this cup from me; yet, not what I want, but what you want' (Mark 14:36). Jesus chose for our sakes to calm and quieten His soul and find security in the eternal love and purposes of His Father. He allowed himself to be betrayed with a traitor's kiss and led to a mocking trial and cruel beatings. 'When he was abused, he did not return abuse; when he suffered, he did not threaten; but he entrusted himself to the one who judges justly' (1 Peter 2:23). He went forward to suffering in quiet obedience to

---

[9] Luke 22:44. See Jim Bishop, *The Day Christ Died* (Glasgow: Fontana Books, William Collins Son & Co Ltd, 1959), p208.

His Father and acceptance of His mission of reconciliation, placing His firm and assured hope in His Father's love and promises knowing that He would not be abandoned to the grave.[10]

Jesus told His followers to place their hope in Him (v3)

Every time Jesus had spoken to His disciples about His forthcoming death, He had told them also that He would rise again on the third day. Only a few hours previously, He had said to them, 'A little while, and you will no longer see me, and again a little while, and you will see me' (John 16:16). As he shared the cup of the new covenant with them at the Last Supper, He said to them, 'I tell you, I will never again drink of this fruit of the vine until that day when I drink it new with you in my Father's kingdom' (Matthew 26:29). A day is to come when Jesus will sit at table with His people, sharing a banquet of rich food:

> On this mountain the LORD of hosts will make for all peoples
> A feast of rich food, a feast of well-matured wines, of rich food filled with marrow, of well-matured wines strained clear …
> he will swallow up death for ever.
> Then the Lord GOD will wipe away the tears from all faces,
> and the disgrace of his people he will take away from all the earth,
> for the LORD has spoken.
> It will be said on that day,

---

[10] Psalm 16:10.

Lo, this is our God; we have waited for him, so that
he might save us.
This is the LORD for whom we have waited;
let us be glad and rejoice in his salvation.
(Isaiah 25:6, 8-9)

By His acceptance of His Father's will, we can wait
hopefully, at ease and calm, with the assurance that all
God's purposes find their 'Yes' in Christ.[11]

Wait, Israel, for GOD. Wait with hope.
Hope now; hope always!
(Psalm 131:3, *The Message*)

Praying Psalm 131 as a follower of Jesus

Discovering the sheer wonder of our Lord, His wisdom,
glory, sovereignty, power and love, we can choose to put
aside the anger we have directed at Him. We can choose
to back away from the pride that has dominated our lives
and held the Lord at bay as we remained in charge of our
own lives. We can choose to cease questioning the
purposes of God, which are always higher than our ways
and thinking. Finally, we can choose to place ourselves
under the tender care and protection of the Lord, resting
like a satisfied and contented child in its mother's arms. In
other words, as Alec Motyer puts it, 'If my "soul" is to be
"quelled" and "silenced", it is up to me to see to it',[12] a
choice which can and will only be made as we bow in the
presence of the Lord.

---

[11] 2 Corinthians 1:20.

[12] Alec Motyer, *Journey, Psalms for Pilgrim People* (Nottingham, Inter-
Varsity Press, 2009), p117.

Like the psalmist, we start by talking to the Lord about ourselves. We tell Him that we are no longer angry with Him, that we have come to the end of our pride and arrogance, that we will not occupy ourselves any more with matters that are too great or wonderful for us, and that we have calmed our soul and found contentment. Face to face with the Lord's holiness and sovereign love, we realise that He is the God who always has been, who is always present with His people, and who will be eternally constantly faithful as God to His people.

> How wonderful, how beautiful, the sight of Thee must be,
> Thine endless wisdom, boundless power, and aweful purity! ...
> O how I fear Thee, living God, with deepest, tenderest fears,
> and worship Thee with trembling hope and penitential tears![13]

Let us look at these choices in more detail.

As we have seen, the bleakness and despair of the psalmist in the previous psalm could easily have led to a heart that was lifted up in anger against God. When things do not go the way we hoped or prayed, and when the ways of God seem unfathomable, frustration and anger can well up at the core of our being. Scripture tells of people like Cain, Jonah and Jeremiah, who became angry because of their frustration that God had not acted according to their understanding. In Psalm 4, David

---

[13] F W Faber (1814-63), *My God, How Wonderful Thou Art* (extracts from verses 3 and 4).

realised how near he was to anger against his Lord after he had been shamed and lied to by those close to him. Realising that he was only a step away from putting himself on a level with God and claiming to know better than his Lord, trust in his Lord's sovereignty won the day; anger was abated and restful sleep followed.

The problem of human pride can be traced right back to Genesis 3, where Adam and Eve, created in the image of God, took it upon themselves to state that they knew better than their Creator. Pride takes root as we presume that we are wiser and more knowledgeable than God and that we can plan our lives without reference to His purposes for us. Trust is the opposite, admitting that when we come to the Lord, we are coming to the One who is utterly trustworthy and whose ownership of our lives is indisputable. The moment we say 'Our Father', we are rejecting our pride and haughtiness and making the choice of entrusting our lives to Him who cares for us and loves us far beyond our understanding or anything we deserve.

The pain of life's experiences, our own mistakes and misguided decisions, as well as the consequences of living in a world riddled with moral decay, can all lead to incessant questions: 'Why has God allowed this to happen to me?' 'If there's a loving God, how could this possibly have happened?' As these questions well up from our pain and darkness, we remember that Jesus also cried out, 'Why?' when He was distanced from His Father by our sin and judgement. Trusting in God is not a guarantee that we will live a life that brooks no such questions. We learn to cope as these questions assault us as our trust in the eternal, creating, loving Father grows.

Margaret Clarkson, the American hymn-writer, described how hard this was for her. Her early years with unloving parents who divorced when she was only twelve left her struggling to find answers:

> Helplessness, hopelessness, rage, frustration, despair, the compulsion to give up and seek cessation from pain in the darkness of death – I knew them all. Despite the reality of a Christian commitment from which I never wavered for a moment, I spent years struggling to find any real meaning in life as I had to live it. How well I know the 'Why?' of human anguish! I found my answers in the Word of God, but not before I was well into my forties, and not without much pain. Slowly but surely the Holy Spirit began to make real to me the teaching of the Scriptures concerning the sovereignty of God and its meaning for my life. Gradually I came to understand something of God's over-arching purpose for His children and His ways of bringing it about. Slowly I began to learn to look beyond my immediate situation to God's ultimate purpose for my life, and doing so I gradually found peace. As my knowledge and understanding of the Scriptures increased, so did my assurance and my spiritual growth.[14]

The choice of Psalm 131 is that readiness to place ourselves under the tender care and protection of the Lord, which

---

[14] Margaret Clarkson, *Destined for Glory: The Meaning of Suffering* (Grand Rapids, MI: William B Eerdmans Publishing Company, 1983), ppviii-ix.

leads to the calmness and quietness of our souls, as a child is content in its mother's arms. Although we ourselves must make this choice, the transformation in our lives will only come about as we allow the Holy Spirit to invade our whole being, so that we know 'the breadth and length and height and depth' of the 'love of Christ' (Ephesians 3:18-19).

The choice of the psalmist worked out in our lives and the arrival of hope are the results of the ministry and guidance of the Holy Spirit. It is He who brings hope as the Father's love is poured into our lives, enabling us slowly but surely to become more like Christ.

As I conclude this chapter, I cannot escape the fact that there are so many in life who face storms that batter and who are in no position to make the choices outlined above. I am thinking of, for example, the adult struggling with the confusion and disorientation of dementia, or the person who suffers the pain of extreme depression which suppresses any ability to make such choices. If their lives, like the psalmist, are to be calmed and quietened, how can they make these choices? What has this psalm to say for these people? The answer surely lies with those of us who can stand with them and pray for them. We must bring them to the throne of grace where Jesus lives to intercede. Crying out to Him in our helplessness, we entrust those for whom we pray to the mercy and loving purposes of the Lord.

Responding

Romans 8:14-16 tells us that it is a work of the Holy Spirit to teach us to call God our Father. When we find that prayer is difficult, we can ask for the help of the Holy Spirit. Realising that we are sons and daughters of our heavenly Father is one of the most important steps on the road to learning to trust Him.

Learning to trust the Lord in the face of suffering, as Margaret Clarkson discovered, can be a long, slow journey. Can you identify with her in your own journey?

I wrote in the last section about those who cannot choose to entrust themselves into the care and protection of the Lord. Do you know someone like this for whom you can pray? Or, if this describes you, do you know someone you trust, with whom you are able to share and pray?

13
Psalm 132
Praying on a Grand Scale

¹ O LORD, remember in David's favour
all the hardships he endured;
² how he swore to the LORD
and vowed to the Mighty One of Jacob,
³ 'I will not enter my house
or get into my bed;
⁴ I will not give sleep to my eyes
or slumber to my eyelids,
⁵ until I find a place for the LORD,
a dwelling-place for the Mighty One of Jacob.'
⁶ We heard of it in Ephrathah;
we found it in the fields of Jaar.
⁷ 'Let us go to his dwelling-place;
let us worship at his footstool.'
⁸ Rise up, O LORD, and go to your resting-place,
you and the ark of your might.
⁹ Let your priests be clothed with righteousness,
and let your faithful shout for joy.
¹⁰ For your servant David's sake
do not turn away the face of your anointed one.
¹¹ The LORD swore to David a sure oath
from which he will not turn back:
'One of the sons of your body

I will set on your throne.
12 If your sons keep my covenant
and my decrees that I shall teach them,
their sons also, for evermore,
shall sit on your throne.'
13 For the LORD has chosen Zion;
he has desired it for his habitation:
14 'This is my resting-place for ever;
here I will reside, for I have desired it.
15 I will abundantly bless its provisions;
I will satisfy its poor with bread.
16 Its priests I will clothe with salvation,
and its faithful will shout for joy.
17 There I will cause a horn to sprout up for David;
I have prepared a lamp for my anointed one.
18 His enemies I will clothe with disgrace,
but on him, his crown will gleam.'

Introducing Psalm 132

The Lord is the God who has covenanted to be always present with His people, and Psalm 132 celebrates that commitment of the Lord throughout their past and into the future. The pilgrims who sang this song knew that their journey would not be complete until they had reached the temple in Jerusalem and worshipped there in the presence of the Lord.

Psalm 132 climbs to its summit in verses 13 and 14 by means of three stories about David in verses 1 to 12. Reaching the summit, the psalmist affirms the covenant of the Lord to be eternally present with His people. The conclusion of the psalm describes the panorama from the summit of all that lies ahead for the Lord's king and His people (vv15-18).

Climbing to the summit (vv1-12)

The first story: David's determination to build the temple (vv1-5)

When King David was living in Jerusalem in palatial luxury, he realised that something had to be done about building a house for his Lord in his capital. For many years, the Ark of the Covenant had been in a tent where a priest called Abinadab lived in Kiriath-jearim on the border between Israelite and Philistine country.[1] The psalmist records that David 'swore to the LORD' that he would put this right, whatever it cost him (vv2-5). But it was not to be. Nathan the prophet, who had been party to the original discussions, came to David the next morning with the news that the Lord had spoken to him about these plans. It would be Solomon, David's son, who would build the house for the Lord.

Reassured by this word from the Lord, David set to and began the necessary preparations. There was to be no luxurious living or sleep until he had brought the Ark to Jerusalem. The Chronicler describes the enormous efforts he went to so that he could pass on to his son Solomon all the plans and a vast treasury of resources from his own personal fortune for the building of the temple, the house of the Lord.[2] He was determined that the Lord's glory would be manifested in Jerusalem through the building of the temple.

---

[1] 1 Samuel 7:1.

[2] 1 Chronicles 22:14; chapters 28–29.

173

These opening verses are a plea that the Lord would remember His promise to David and all the 'hardships' that David endured in making it possible for the house of the Lord to be built.

The second story: The Philistines and the Ark (vv6-10)

The psalmist puts himself in David's place when he decided to bring the Ark from Kiriath-jearim[3] to his newly established capital of Jerusalem. David's action was reinforced by memories of stories he had been told in his early years while living as the youngest of eight brothers in Ephrathah, another name for the district of Bethlehem. In the days of Samuel the judge, the Philistines had defeated the Israelites in battle and stolen the Ark of the Covenant. (The Ark was a wooden box about 4 feet long, 2 feet wide and 2 feet deep, built by Moses according to instructions given by God. It originally contained the stone tablets on which were written the Ten Commandments given to Moses by God on Mount Sinai, a jar of manna and Aaron's rod that budded: all clear reminders of the Lord's commands, His provision and His actions in saving His people. By the time of Solomon's dedication of the temple, only the stone tablets remained.[4] The Ark of the Covenant was revered by the Israelites as the visible symbol and testimony of God's promises and presence.[5]) But wherever the Philistines took the Ark,

---

[3] Jaar (132:6), (meaning *wood, forest*) is quite possibly a shortened form of Kiriath-jearim (meaning *city of* woods) describing the forested land surrounding round the town. (See Cuthbert C Keet, *A Study of the Psalms of Ascents* (London, The Mitre Press, 1969), p92.)

[4] 1 Kings 8:9.

[5] Exodus 25:10-22.

there were disasters and illnesses and they were forced to return their hard-won prize to their enemies. These dramatic events, recounted in 1 Samuel 4–6, and the Ark's eventual return to Kiriath-jearim must have ranked highly among the tales told to youngsters. King David's first attempt to bring the Ark to Jerusalem went disastrously wrong, but he succeeded on his second attempt. The great rejoicing that rang out across the city as the Ark was placed in the tent that David had prepared for it is described here. The Ark of the Covenant, the surety of the Lord's presence with the Children of Israel, was once again in the midst of His people.

The third story: Nathan tells David of the Lord's covenant (vv11-12)

Up to this point in the psalm the psalmist has been speaking, but now the Lord speaks about His covenant with David, promising that his throne will be an eternal throne. We have already seen how the prophet Nathan told David that his son would be the one who would build the house of the Lord. Now the Lord spoke through Nathan again about far greater matters! The continuity of King David's succession was secure, and his successors would be honoured and loved by the Lord as a father loves his son. The authority and rule of David's kingdom was assured by an eternal covenant:

> The LORD declares to you that the LORD himself will establish a house for you: when your days are over and you rest with your ancestors, I will raise up your offspring to succeed you, your own flesh and blood, and I will establish his kingdom. He is the

one who will build a house for my Name, and I will establish the throne of his kingdom for ever. I will be his father, and he shall be my son ... Your house and your kingdom shall endure for ever before me; your throne will be established for ever.

(2 Samuel 7:11-14, 16, NIVUK)

This was a vital promise to the Lord's people, which they came to understand as the promise of a future king, the Messiah, who would establish an eternal kingdom and rule in peace and equity:

authority rests upon his shoulders;
and he is named
Wonderful Counsellor, Mighty God,
Everlasting Father, Prince of Peace.
His authority shall grow continually,
and there shall be endless peace
for the throne of David and his kingdom.
He will establish and uphold it
with justice and with righteousness
from this time onwards and for evermore.
The zeal of the LORD of hosts will do this.

(Isaiah 9:6-7)

Standing on the summit (vv13-14)

The mountain has been climbed and it as if the psalmist places a flag on the summit to make his point. What the Lord had promised on the ascent has been fulfilled! Zion (which, as we said earlier, can mean the city of Jerusalem or the Lord's people) is now in reality the place where the Lord lives. That was His desired purpose, and pilgrims arriving in Jerusalem knew that His oath sworn to David had been fulfilled. When Solomon had finished building his father's planned temple, the Chronicler tells us that following the King's prayer, which used words which this psalm recalls,[6] fire descended and the glory of the Lord filled the temple.[7] It was in no way a temporary fulfilment. The Lord's certain covenant was, and remains, that He will rest and remain with His people for ever.

The view from the summit (vv15-18)

The Lord had clearly promised to be present with His people, but it was difficult to see the fulfilment of that promise in the events that followed over hundreds of years. The story of the Lord's people in the years after Solomon's reign and their repeated refusal to remain faithful to their Lord meant that Jerusalem, with its temple, was eventually destroyed by the Babylonian army in 586BC, and the Ark of the Covenant was lost.

But the Lord's faithfulness to His covenant would never be undone by His people's faithlessness. His unchanging and steadfast love is forever. Even though disobedience would often rule the day, the Lord declared that His eternal purpose to be present among His people could never be thwarted. It would be fulfilled completely at the coming of the Messiah, His anointed One, who would usher in a time of extravagant provision for all. He will clothe priests with salvation and His people will 'shout for joy'. The Messiah will reign in great power (the horn is a symbol of victorious power) and will be a lamp bringing light into a dark world. As the Lord's anointed

---

[6] 2 Chronicles 6:41; Psalm 132:8-10.

[7] 2 Chronicles 7:1-2; see Exodus 40:34-35.

One, He will vanquish all His enemies and be crowned with radiant glory.

The panorama is breathtaking! The Lord has made a covenant with His people: the promise of an eternal kingdom under the reign of a Messiah who will rule in justice and righteousness![8]

Jesus and Psalm 132

Jesus is the new King David (vv11-12)

A few days after Jesus' triumphant entry into Jerusalem on Palm Sunday, He was teaching in the temple courts. He reminded the scribes and Pharisees of the cries of the crowd that had welcomed Him into the city and challenged them with a question: 'How can the scribes say that the Messiah is the son of David?' (Mark 12:35). Jesus was referring to Psalm 110 where David speaks the word of the Lord to a king to be installed as his successor:[9] 'The word of Yahweh to my Sovereign One: Sit enthroned at my right hand' (Psalm 110:1[10]). This King will clearly be a king greater than David: his 'Lord'.

The scribes and Pharisees were thrown into more confusion when Jesus then asked them to explain how the expected Messiah could possibly be the son of David as well as being David's Lord. As Jesus confounded His critics, He was declaring that the Messiah would reign as

[8] Psalm 89:19-29 describes the rule of this successor to King David.
[9] It is vital to note here (Mark 12:36) that Jesus said that David's writing of Psalm 110 was inspired by the Holy Spirit.
[10] Translation from Alec Motyer, *Psalms by the Day*, p314.

King at the right hand of God over a universal and eternal kingdom.[11]

The point is made finally in the penultimate words of Jesus in the New Testament: 'I am the root and the descendant of David, the bright morning star' (Revelation 22:16). Jesus was both the source and continuation of David's kingship, reigning as King of kings with a radiance (132:18) like that of the morning star.

The zeal of Jesus for His Father's house (vv1-10)

David was determined to build the temple for the Lord. Looking back on the life, passion and resurrection of Jesus, John comments on the cleansing of the temple at the beginning of Jesus' ministry: 'His disciples remembered that it was written, "Zeal for your house will consume me"' (John 2:17). Jesus had cleared the physical temple, His Father's house, of money changers and sellers of animals, declaring that if this temple were to be destroyed, He would build it again within three days! John explains that the temple Jesus was speaking of was His body; it would be destroyed in crucifixion and raised up again in three days.

John had already stated this in the prologue to his Gospel when he made specific reference to the tent built to house the Ark of the Covenant in the wilderness wanderings of the Children of Israel. The Word, who was God and who was with God in the beginning, became flesh, and they saw His glory as He pitched His tent

---

[11] This is developed by Peter in his sermon at Pentecost. See Acts 2:29-36.

among them.[12] Previously the Lord had been present in the tabernacle where the Ark rested and in the temple in Jerusalem. But now, says John, everything has changed. God's presence and His glory are fully revealed in Jesus Christ, the eternal Word made flesh, dwelling (tabernacling, templing) among us.

David Ford makes the point that the title of Jesus as 'the Nazarene' that Pilate had nailed to the cross:

> might well have been a royal messianic title associated with rebuilding the temple, in line with John's association of the death and resurrection of Jesus with the destruction and rebuilding of the temple (in [John] 2:13-25, during this Gospel's first Passover in Jerusalem). If so it serves to emphasize still further ... the identification Jesus with the temple.[13]

In His life, Jesus declared that He was the true temple where God was fully present (John 1:14; 2:19-21). That truth was reinforced in His passion.

The kingdom and reign of the Messiah (vv13-18)

As King Jesus, the Lord's anointed One, prayed this psalm, He would have looked ahead to both humiliation and exaltation. First to come was the agony, the trial and crucifixion as the Son of God humbled Himself to death. The hardships, troubling and weakness of great King David were far surpassed by the sufferings of his Greater

---

[12] John 1:14.

[13] David Ford, *The Gospel of John, a Theological Commentary* (Grand Rapids, MI: Baker Academic, 2021), p376.

Son. Then, through His self-giving sacrifice and His triumphant resurrection, Jesus would ascend to be crowned with a radiant crown to reign with supreme authority over an eternal kingdom of righteousness.

The King to come will administer a kingdom of abundance for all, with a rich banquet for all nations and all peoples: 'Many will come from east and west and will eat with Abraham and Isaac and Jacob in the kingdom of heaven' (Matthew 8:11).

The King to come will clothe His priests with righteousness, and the people will rejoice and sing! It is the risen Jesus Christ who has forgiven and redeemed us and who has 'made us to be a kingdom, priests serving his God and Father, to him be glory and dominion for ever and ever. Amen' (Revelation 1:6).[14]

The King to come will reign over His enemies, as did King David, but in a far greater manner and with power that is infinite and immeasurable. His light will shine brighter than the sun, banishing darkness and sin. King Jesus will wear a crown of radiant glory and honour.[15]

The Lord's promise to David was given the Amen in Jesus Christ. The Lord's everlasting covenant promises are completely fulfilled, and every promise made to King David is complete in Jesus Christ.

Praying Psalm 132 as a follower of Jesus

Psalm 132 encourages us to pray on a grand scale as we affirm and celebrate the purposes of God in Christ in time and eternity! The psalmist prayed that the Lord would

---

[14] See also 1 Peter 2:5-11.

[15] Hebrews 2:7-9.

remember David, his determination and the hardships he endured in order to build a house for the Lord. We pray in the name of Jesus because of all the self-denial, self-emptying and affliction He endured in order to establish the new covenant, guaranteeing that He would be with us for ever by His Holy Spirit.[16] The more fully we realise the nature of the covenant that the Father has established with us in Christ, the more confident we will be in our praying.

Therefore, it is important that we look carefully at what is meant by the term 'covenant' in Scripture. A covenant is generally understood to be a binding agreement between two parties, but in the Bible a covenant established by the Lord is always a one-sided agreement, established without reference to any other party.

God makes His covenant with us purely by His own decision, stemming from the unfathomable depths of His love for those He has created. The Lord chooses with whom He will establish His covenant. He seals it by sacrifice at a time He chooses. He established His covenant with Abram, Moses and David on behalf of His people. He told Isaiah, Jeremiah and Ezekiel that He was going to make a new covenant with His people.[17] Zechariah, the father of John the Baptist, praised the God of Israel because He had remembered the covenant made with Abraham and was now raising up a strong king of salvation from the house of David.[18] These were not separate or individual covenants. Whenever God said to

---

[16] John 14:16.

[17] Genesis 17:2; Exodus 34: 27; Psalm 89:3; Isaiah 55:3; Jeremiah 31:33; Ezekiel 37:26.

[18] Luke 1:68-73.

his Old Testament people that He was making a covenant with them, He was affirming the original covenant He had made with Abraham. Every sacrifice in the Old Testament relates back to the original covenant with Abraham,[19] and looks forward to the new covenant, promised by the prophets and made by Jesus Christ, sealed with His all-sufficient, atoning sacrifice on the cross.

This new covenant was the result of a decision made by the three Persons of the Trinity before the foundation of the world on behalf of sinful men and women. It was and remains forever an undeserved offer of grace because of and through Jesus Christ.

When He sat at table in the Upper Room with His friends, He gave bread to them, saying that they were to eat it in remembrance of Him.[20] Then He took the cup of wine and shared it with them, telling them that it was the blood of the new covenant 'poured out for many for the forgiveness of sins' (Matthew 26:28). In other words, Jesus Himself is the bread that was eaten at every Jewish Passover in remembrance of God's deliverance of His people from Egypt. Jesus Himself is the blood shed for the forgiveness of sins in every Old Testament sacrifice. Everything promised in the Old Testament covenant was fulfilled and completed in Him, Son of God and Son of Man, incarnate, crucified, died, risen, ascended and glorified.

Paul states that this new covenant is secured in us by the Holy Spirit. When we trust in Jesus Christ, he says, the Holy Spirit seals what the Father has done for us in Christ.

---

[19] Genesis 15.
[20] Luke 22:19.

The word used for that act of sealing is loaded with significance.[21] It means that our salvation is authenticated in Christ beyond doubt and marked by the gift of the Holy Spirit with our new owner's mark of identification for complete protection, now and into eternity.

Our presence at the Messiah's banquet is assured. We will eat and drink, rejoicing in the dazzling presence of the radiant King, who will have defeated all His enemies and established His rule of justice and peace.

Responding

Every time we pray, like the psalmist, we stand on the ground of this new covenant that has been established so completely in Jesus Christ. Every time we pray 'Lord, remember,' with the psalmist, we are entrusting ourselves to the embrace of God's eternal covenant of grace and love held out to us in His Son, Jesus Christ.

This encourages us to pray on a grand scale as we remember the purposes of God in Christ in time and eternity! You were chosen in Christ 'before the foundation of the world' (Ephesians 1:4), secured by the gift of the Holy Spirit when you believed in Christ and were kept as God's possession into eternity. Read, meditate on and pray through Ephesians 1:3-14.

Our God is 'a walking God',[22] who has promised to walk beside us every step of our pilgrimage. Why do you think we forget this so easily?

---

[21] See 2 Corinthians 1:22; Ephesians 1:13; 4:30.
[22] Samuel Terrien, *The Elusive Presence* (New York: Harper and Row, 1978), p170.

14
Psalm 133
Relationships on the Journey

¹ How very good and pleasant it is
when kindred live together in unity!
² It is like the precious oil on the head,
running down upon the beard,
on the beard of Aaron,
running down over the collar of his robes.
³ It is like the dew of Hermon,
which falls on the mountains of Zion.
For there the LORD ordained his blessing,
life for evermore.

Introducing Psalm 133

We can imagine the scene! Worshippers are converging on Jerusalem from all over Galilee and Judaea. The journey is almost over. Families and friends from different communities are meeting up with old friends from previous festival celebrations. There may have been pressures on the way which have resulted in conflicts, but now these are put to rest as the city of Jerusalem comes into sight.

Psalm 133 is like a conversation between two friends about their experiences on the way to Jerusalem. The group in front of them always seem to be arguing. There is a lot of shouting and verbal abuse. The faces of many of the youngsters in the group are often pained and tear-streaked. It is not a happy party.

Behind the two pilgrims is another group who have learned the art of travelling together, supporting each other, sharing the load, and constantly encouraging and affirming one another. Youngsters and older members of the group are smiling, conversing and laughing together. This group is a happy party!

The two friends have been watching these groups over the last few days of their pilgrimage, and one says to the other, 'It's so good when people get on with each other!'

Then the conversation seems to take a strange turn. Back comes the reply, 'It's like costly anointing oil flowing down head and beard, flowing down Aaron's beard, flowing down the collar of his priestly robes.'

To which the first replies, 'It's like the dew on Mount Hermon flowing down the slopes of Zion. Yes, that's where GOD commands the blessing, ordains eternal life.'[1]

This might seem a strange conversation to us, but these two friends were using images familiar to any pilgrim en route for Jerusalem! We will try to unwrap these images.

A lost ideal – the first statement (v1)

Look, says the psalmist, see 'how good' and how 'pleasant' it is when people live in harmony.

The word 'good' here echoes the creation account of Genesis 1 where God pronounces repeatedly that His creation is 'good'. On the sixth day, when everything else

---

[1] Psalm 133:2-3 (*The Message*).

had been created, God created us in His own image to live in perfect unity with each other and with God Himself. We were created, states Darrell Johnson:

> to reflect the relational nature of God. The living God is a Community, a Fellowship. At the centre of all things is a Relationship, and we were made *by* the Relationship, *for* the Relationship, to live *in* relationship. This is the most fundamental thing the Scriptures tell us about being human.[2]

But the centre of all things was shattered when Adam and Eve chose to ignore the commands of God and put their own desires first. Things changed immediately as their relationships with God and with each other were destroyed. The good and pleasant land of Eden became a far-off and unreachable country because of disobedience. Living in good and pleasant unity tragically became a fleeting dream from a distant past. There was no way back to unity and togetherness. An angel with a flaming sword guarded the way back to Eden and the tree of life.[3]

How wonderful, says the psalmist, if the relationships once known in Eden could be experienced in our lives once again.

The picture of anointing (v2)

The conversation continues. If we knew this unity and fellowship, it would be as if we were anointed with oil.

---

[2] Darrell Johnson, *The Story of All Stories: Genesis 1–11* (Vancouver: Regent College Publishing, 2019), p38 (author's italics). Used with the author's permission.

[3] Genesis 3:24.

There are two kinds of anointing in the Old Testament referred to in this conversation. One is an anointing of welcome and the other is an anointing to the office of priest or king.

The first half of verse 2 refers to the anointing of the head with olive oil, scented with sweet-smelling spices. This was a sign of welcome, given on arrival to a family member or loved friend arriving home. Psalm 23:5 tells of the fatigued traveller whose head is anointed with oil as well as being provided with food and drink. Ecclesiastes 9:7-9 speaks of oil poured on the head as a sign of joy and good relationships, , while Isaiah 61:3 states that the gift of 'the oil of gladness' will be given 'to those who mourn in Zion'.

To be anointed with oil is to be welcomed into a loving community, a place of forgiveness and healing.

Then, suddenly, in the second half of verse 2, Aaron, the brother of Moses, is brought into the picture. The anointing referred to now is that of consecration to priesthood. Aaron was the high priest who represented the Lord's people when he went into the Holy of Holies in the tabernacle to make atonement for sin. Shortly after leaving Egypt, the Children of Israel arrived at Mount Sinai and Moses met with God on the mountain. The Lord spoke to him and instructed him to tell His people that they were his 'treasured possession out of all the peoples … a priestly kingdom and a holy nation' (Exodus 19:5-6). Aaron's ministry as high priest was representative of this priesthood, which was given to all the Children of Israel. They were called, as are all the Lord's people, to be a priestly, peace-making people, both among themselves and to the nations around. Their commitment in this God-given task was to bring the knowledge of forgiveness, peace and the Lord's blessing to all people.

> To be anointed with oil is to be marked out as a priest. Living together means seeing the oil flow over the head, down the face, through the beard, onto the shoulders of the other – and when I see that I know my brother, my sister is my priest. When we see the other as God's anointed, our relationships are profoundly affected.[4]

Anointing with oil is a doubly rich picture which speaks of unity, welcome and acceptance, as well as the priestly responsibility of the Lord's people to be bringers of forgiveness and peace to each other and those around.

The picture of the dew of Mount Hermon (v3a)

The conversation has stirred vivid pictures in the minds of the pilgrims! Throughout the Old Testament, dew is a picture of blessing,[5] and the picture here imagines the dew of Mount Hermon falling on dry and rocky Mount Zion. One traveller to Mount Hermon in the nineteenth century wrote:

> More copious dew we never experienced. Everything was drenched with it, and the tents were small protection. The under sides of our

---

[4] Peterson, *A Long Obedience in the Same Direction*, p175.
[5] For the association between dew and the Lord's blessing in the Old Testament, see Genesis 27:28; Deuteronomy 33:28; Isaiah 26:19; Hosea 14:5.

macintosh sheets were in water ... dew drops were hanging everywhere.[6]

The picture is of a resident of Jerusalem waking up one morning to discover that the grass is green and flowers are bursting into bloom after an exceptionally heavy dew, where before there had only been dry and barren ground. If the Lord's people were to discover how to live in unity, it would bring refreshment far beyond anything they could expect or dream of. It would be a sure sign of His extravagant blessing, as if the abundance of dew that fell upon Mount Hermon were to fall upon Mount Zion.

A final observation (v3b)

Only the Lord could command such blessing; it springs from Him alone. The Lord's people can live together in unity and love. It is a gift appointed and ordained by the Lord Himself. It is nothing less than the restoration of Eden. Once bestowed, the Lord will walk and talk with His people and that divine, eternal accompaniment will transform and bless all our relationships.

Jesus and Psalm 133

As Jesus approached Jerusalem with His disciples, His heart was heavy. He knew that in spite of all His teaching and example over the past three years, there was misunderstanding and disunity among the twelve.

Approaching Jericho, Jesus took them aside and explained what would happen when they arrived in Jerusalem. He would be arrested, mocked, insulted and

---

[6] H B Tristram, *The Land of Israel* (London: SPCK, 1865), pp603-604.

spat on. Then He would be killed, but on the third day He would rise again. Luke comments that they did not understand any of this; they simply did not know what He was talking about.[7]

Disunity among the twelve reared its ugly head as they started up the road from Jericho to Jerusalem. James and John, to the annoyance of the other disciples, asked Jesus if they could sit on His right and His left in the glory of His kingdom. His reply started with a rebuke: 'You do not know what you are asking' (Mark 10:35-41).

Spending time at the house of Mary, Martha and Lazarus in Bethany during Holy Week must have been a refuge in the storm for Jesus. It was a home where 'his heart was open and readily responded to the delights of human association, and bound itself to others in a happy fellowship'.[8] It was 'good and pleasant' for our Lord to experience such unity and fellowship, and He longed to see a similar unity when He gathered with His disciples in the Upper Room. He had 'eagerly desired to eat this Passover' (Luke 22:15) with them and He was determined to show them that His love for them was unchanging and unending.[9]

But disunity prevailed. There was an argument among the twelve about which of them was the most important. Then Judas Iscariot left the room, having agreed a sum of money for the betrayal of his Master. Peter stated his determination to follow Jesus come what may, but that was later pushed beyond the limit by the searching

---

[7] Luke 18:31-34.
[8] Warfield, *The Person and Work of Christ*, p106.
[9] John 13:1.

questions of a servant girl.[10] Jesus must have longed for His disciples to 'live together in unity', but it seemed like a dream. Or was it?

These confused disciples were shortly to listen to Jesus praying for them and for all who would follow them as a result of their witness. He prayed that their unity would be like the unity He shared with his Father:

> I ask not only on behalf of these, but also on behalf of those who will believe in me through their word, that they may all be one. As you, Father, are in me and I am in you, may they also be in us, so that the world may believe that you have sent me. The glory that you have given me I have given them, so that they may be one, as we are one, I in them and you in me, that they may become completely one, so that the world may know that you have sent me and have loved them even as you have loved me.
> (John 17:20-23)

Before creation, the Father and the Son determined to create a forgiven and reconciled people, and Jesus was praying here for the fulfilment of this divine purpose. In dying, He would be the anointed High Priest and Mediator, standing between the Father and His people by virtue of His sinless life and sin-bearing death. By His life, death and resurrection and by His giving of the Holy Spirit, Jesus holds out the possibility of living at peace with the Father and in unity and peace with those around us.

---

[10] Mark 14:27-31, 66-72.

Can this prayer be answered? Most certainly, because of the Priest who made it possible for us to be reconciled to the Father and live as forgiven people. However, the responsibility of making that a reality lies fairly and squarely on our shoulders, as Jesus made quite clear in the Lord's Prayer. After teaching his disciples to ask for forgiveness only when they had forgiven others, He added:

> In prayer there is a connection between what God does and what you do. You can't get forgiveness from God, for instance, without also forgiving others. If you refuse to do your part, you cut yourself off from God's part.
> Matthew 6:14-15 (*The Message*)

How, then, do we pray this psalm for ourselves?

Praying Psalm 133 as a follower of Jesus

Journeying towards the heavenly city, we are acutely aware of our damaged and fractured relationships. How wonderful it would be if we could always walk in unity with those around us. There is a hint that this longing could become a reality when we read of the early church: 'All who believed were together and had all things in common', 'The whole group of those who believed were of one heart and soul' (Acts 2:44; 4:32).

But tragically, division in churches and between Christians, over doctrine, worship, leadership styles, authority structures and many other areas, is rampant. Relationships in families and communities are often stretched to breaking point with unresolved divisions and declarations of unending enmity.

Faced with all this, we must look at the Master, who took a towel and washed His disciples' feet. 'There is no instance in either Jewish or Greco-Roman sources of a superior washing the feet of an inferior.'[11] A rabbi would expect his disciples to wash his feet, but disciples would never wash the feet of their equals. Jesus established a vital principle for the Christian disciple as He laid aside outer garments and dignity, knelt in front of the disciples and washed the grime and dust from their tired feet. What He did was no more and no less than what He had taught:

> You know that the rulers of the Gentiles lord it over them, and their great ones are tyrants over them. It will not be so among you; but whoever wishes to be great among you must be your servant, and whoever wishes to be first among you must be your slave; just as the Son of Man came not to be served but to serve, and to give his life a ransom for many.' (Matthew 20:25-28)

Later, in the Upper Room, Jesus told His disciples that one of them would betray Him. What He then told John, who was next to Him, must have shocked him: 'It is the one to whom I give this piece of bread when I have dipped it in the dish' (John 13:26). The Eastern tradition of sharing one's bread with the honoured guest was for His betrayer.

---

[11] Chris Thomas, 'Footwashing in John 13 and the Johannine Community', PhD dissertation, Sheffield University, quoted by D A Carson, *The Gospel According to John* (Downers Grove, IL: IVP, 1991), p462.

Love and forgiveness were held out to the very end as Judas Iscariot, sitting next to Jesus, took the gift of bread.

Hanging in pain on the cross, forgiveness was given when none was asked for, as Jesus prayed for those who crucified Him: 'Father, forgive them; for they do not know what they are doing' (Luke 23:34).

We are called to such forgiveness. It is difficult and costly, sacrificial in the extreme. Psalm 133 holds out the possibility that such forgiveness can actually become a reality.

There must be an anointing. The Father welcomes us into His family with our brother, the Lord Jesus:

> God, who is rich in mercy, out of the great love with which he loved us even when we were dead through our trespasses, made us alive together with Christ – by grace you have been saved – and raised us up with him and seated us with him in the heavenly places in Christ Jesus.
> (Ephesians 2:4-6)

The One with whom we are seated has scars in His hands, feet and side. Even though it was our sin that caused the death of His Son, the Father forgives us with love that cannot be measured, welcoming and assuring us of our security in Christ.[12]

It is an anointing by a High Priest who is 'holy, blameless, undefiled, separated from sinners, and exalted above the heavens' (Hebrews 7:26). His priestly work of mediation and reconciliation is eternally complete and

---

[12] 2 Corinthians 1:21-22.

effective. It is an anointing by a High Priest who lives to pray continually for those He is bringing to glory.

But we remain acutely aware of the deep pain of our broken relationships and the struggle to forgive. We ask for forgiveness but we struggle to forgive those who have hurt us. Wounds can fester and all too easily the desire wells up within us to ignore or cause pain to the one who has hurt us. How can we who are one with Christ entertain such thoughts and feelings?

This is where the picture of the dew of Mount Hermon has such relevance. As the dew of the Lord's blessing is poured onto our lives, we can gradually reach a place of forgiveness. The Holy Spirit pours the love of God into the depths of our beings and begins to produce within us His fruit of love, patience, kindness and self-control, the very opposite of revenge, hurt and the refusal to forgive.[13] Working deeply within us as we give Him permission, He begins a process of transformation. The desire for revenge can gradually change into a longing for reconciliation, as within us can grow both the will and the ability to forgive. The desire to hurt can be replaced by an emerging love, and the refusal to forgive can be reversed. This is the work of the Holy Spirit, pouring the dew of blessing on the barren, dry ground of our lives and producing growth and fruitfulness.

As the psalm teaches in its conclusion, this is the Lord's work. He commands the blessing. He has united us with His Son and He gives us His Holy Spirit to know and live out that unity. But it is quite possible, says Paul, to grieve the Holy Spirit:

---

[13] See Galatians 5:19-25.

Do not grieve the Holy Spirit of God, with which you were marked with a seal for the day of redemption. Put away from you all bitterness and wrath and anger and wrangling and slander, together with all malice, and be kind to one another, tender-hearted, forgiving one another, as God in Christ has forgiven you.
(Ephesians 4:30-32)

Discord, anger and malice all wound the Holy Spirit. The very fact that the third Person of the blessed Trinity resides within us should instruct and prompt us to glorify Christ in all things and at all times. Knowing and experiencing the love of God, which 'has been poured into our hearts through the Holy Spirit' (Romans 5:5), we are motivated and enabled to show that love to all around us, longing to live with forgiveness and at peace with all people.

Now the ideal of the psalmist and the prayer of our Lord can be answered in full as we allow our whole beings to be drenched with the dew of God's blessing, thus allowing the Holy Spirit to transform us into the image of Christ. It will be answered entirely when Christ comes again, and 'we will be like him, for we will see him as he is' (1 John 3:2). Then blessing will be commanded for eternity!

Responding

Why do you think it can feel more comfortable to hang on to our resentments than to allow ourselves to be 'drenched' by the Holy Spirit?

The first step in the steep stairway of forgiveness is a choice: do I want to forgive? When the desire and the will to forgive are there, it becomes less difficult to move on to the remaining steps. Do you need to ask for the Lord's help in taking this first step?

15
Psalm 134
Arrival!

¹ Come, bless the LORD, all you servants of the LORD,
who stand by night in the house of the LORD!
² Lift up your hands to the holy place,
and bless the LORD.
³ May the LORD, maker of heaven and earth,
bless you from Zion.

Introducing Psalm 134

Setting the scene

The journey is done! You have arrived in Jerusalem for the Passover Festival. The city is bustling with thousands of Jews from all over the known world staying in lodgings, synagogues, religious communities or with friends, sharing their houses or camping in their gardens. Everything has been unpacked, your lodging place is sorted out and Passover preparations are nearly ready. As daylight fades, it is time to walk to the temple for the evening sacrifice.[1] Arriving there, you join with excited crowds of worshippers preparing to worship and bless the Lord.

---

[1] Numbers 28:4; Deuteronomy 16:5-6.

The sheer noise and the wonder of worship in the temple, the dwelling place of the Lord, is overwhelming. It was the goal of your pilgrimage. All the danger, struggles and hardships of the journey are past. You are where you longed to be and your heart is warmed as, together with thousands of others, you remember with thanksgiving the salvation provided by the Lord on that first Passover night in Egypt hundreds of years ago.

Standing in wonder, you wait while the lamb for your Passover meal is sacrificed. The temple resounds to the sounds of the ram's horn and choirs of priests praising the Lord for the deliverance of His people from Egypt. You try to hold in your memory the sights and sounds of everything you see and hear! As the evening sacrifice draws to an end, you leave, carrying the sacrificed lamb provided for your own family Passover celebration. Priests standing on the steps of the temple pronounce the blessing over you:

> The LORD bless you and keep you;
> the LORD make his face to shine upon you, and be gracious to you;
> the LORD lift up his countenance upon you, and give you peace.
> (Numbers 6:24-26)

It is time to walk back to your lodgings along the dark paths. The choirs and the sound of the ram's horn still ring out in the cold night air and, as you return with your friends and family, you sing psalms of praise with glad hearts.

Understanding the psalm

The psalm falls into two distinct sections held together by the word 'bless'. The first section (vv1-2) starts with an invitation to join the throng of worshippers with the word, 'Come'! The worshippers, servants of the promise-keeping Lord, are to bless the Lord, lifting up their hands in blessing.

Then, reading on to the end of the psalm, we discover that He wants to bless us! The same word is used in all three verses. As we bless the Lord (vv1-2), we are called to stand in worshipful and humble gratitude, remembering His acts of mercy and love, and adoring Him for His steadfast, never-failing love. Blessing us (v3), the Lord gives to us from His riches what we lack: forgiveness, protection, accompaniment, grace and peace.

This psalm is for those who have completed their pilgrimage. It is for pilgrims who have found their strength in the Lord as they journeyed through waterless valleys, places of tears and suffering. It is a psalm for pilgrims who have travelled faithfully and obediently and who long with every step to stand and worship in the presence of their Lord.

As these pilgrims bless the Lord they are encouraged to raise their hands as a sign of blessing (v2). The Old Testament reminds us that hands were lifted up when taking an oath or crying out for help. The raising of hands is also a sign of commitment to the One they are blessing.[2]

That brings us to the last verse, where there are two important changes. First, it is the Lord, Creator of heaven

---

[2] Leviticus 9:22; Deuteronomy 32:40; Psalm 28:2; 141:2.

and earth, who blesses now, and, second, the ones He blesses are individuals rather than the whole group of pilgrims. The distinction is lost in our modern English translations, but clear and correct in the older English of the Authorised Version: 'The LORD that made heaven and earth bless thee out of Zion.' As Derek Kidner points out, there is an unequal exchange in this psalm: 'To bless God is to acknowledge gratefully what He is; but to bless man, God must make of him what he is not, and give him what he has not.'[3] Each pilgrim is individually assured of the Lord's blessing in all its fullness. What better conclusion to a long and arduous journey!

Jesus and Psalm 134

We need to look now at some of the events of the Thursday in Holy Week and at Jesus' last evening with His disciples in the Upper Room.

Jesus instructed Peter and John to go and prepare the Passover. On going into Jerusalem, they would meet a man carrying a pitcher of water who would lead them to a house in the city. They were to say to the owner of the house, 'The Teacher asks you, "Where is the guest room, where I may eat the Passover with my disciples?"' (Luke 22:11). He would then take them to a large, furnished room upstairs where they were to make preparations for the meal.

After following these instructions, Peter and John would have gone to the temple for the evening sacrifice as the sun began to set. They took with them a lamb, which they passed over to the priests for the service of worship.

---

[3] Derek Kidner, *Psalms 73–150*, p454.

Receiving back their sacrificed lamb, they would have returned to the Upper Room, where they met with Jesus and the other ten disciples for their Passover celebrations. It is important to note that the Gospel writers do not say that Jesus went to the temple for the evening sacrifice. He was Himself the temple of the Lord, the One in whom all the fullness of God dwelt bodily.[4]

As the evening progressed, Jesus and His disciples would have sung the Hallel Psalms (Psalms 113–118), traditional Passover songs of praise, blessing and thanksgiving, celebrating the Lord's deliverance of the Children of Israel from Egypt. The first one sets the theme for their Passover feast:

> Blessed be the name of the LORD
> from this time on and for evermore.
> From the rising of the sun to its setting
> the name of the LORD is to be praised.
> The LORD is high above all nations,
> and his glory above the heavens.
> (Psalm 113:2-4)

On that darkest of nights, they blessed the Lord as they remembered together His acts of mercy and love in delivering Israel, adoring Him for His steadfast, never-failing love. But they were not worshipping in the temple; their worship was in the very presence of the Lamb of God who would offer Himself as a sacrifice to take away the sin of the world.[5] The lamb prepared for their Passover meal was only a sign of what was to come.

---

[4] Colossians 2:9.

[5] John 1:29; 1 Corinthians 5:7.

While they were eating, Jesus took a loaf of bread, and after blessing it he broke it, gave it to the disciples, and said, 'Take, eat; this is my body.' Then he took a cup, and after giving thanks he gave it to them, saying, 'Drink from it, all of you; for this is my blood of the covenant, which is poured out for many for the forgiveness of sins.
(Matthew 26:26-28)

The broken bread signified His body, soon to be broken by crucifixion as He bore the sin of the whole world. The wine signified His blood poured out in order to seal and establish God's new covenant. The significance of every Old Testament sacrifice was to be fulfilled in Jesus Christ. He was Himself the Passover lamb whose sacrifice and death would atone for the sin of the whole world.

Jesus stood that evening with His disciples and blessed the Lord. As the meal drew to its end, He would have blessed His disciples, before saying to them, 'Rise, let us be on our way' (John 14:31). Together they walked from the Upper Room towards Gethsemane, His betrayal, arrest, trial and crucifixion.

Praying Psalm 134 as a follower of Jesus

Every time we partake of the Lord's Supper, we sit with those disciples in the Upper Room and hear the words of our Saviour: 'This is my body that is for you ... This cup is the new covenant in my blood' (1 Corinthians 11:24-25).

For us, in one sense, it is night, just as it was for the disciples. We are worshipping in between the events of Holy Week and the dawn of the new creation at the return of Christ. In the words of Psalm 130:6, we are waiting for the Lord with a longing that is 'more than those who watch for the morning'. We live in an interim period; the new creation has been inaugurated, but our journey is in the old creation. We walk through a dark world towards a dawn assured by the faithfulness of the One who tells His Church that He is the 'morning star' (Revelation 22:16; 2 Peter 1:19). Till then, we stand as servants of the Lord in the night, blessing the One who by His suffering and resurrection has made the coming dawn a certainty.

To bless the Lord will often be a joyful part of our everyday life. At other times, when suffering clouds the way, it will be hard. We will be able to sing songs of blessing on some occasions. At other times we will rely on 'godly remembrance' (see Psalm 124), or it may be that all we can do is raise our hands in silent supplication, as we commit to our Lord the wounds and pain suffered on our journey. Even this handing over is a blessing, a sign of our deepest trust.

Whatever the circumstances or however dark it may seem, the promise is that we will arrive at Mount Zion. The day will come when all the demonic powers of this dark world and the totality of the spiritual forces of evil that surround us will bow the knee at the name of King Jesus, enthroned with complete authority and majesty at the right hand of the Father.[6] Then we will stand before the Lord, blessing Him as we lift up our hands in His presence. We will know His blessing upon us, the blessing of our covenant-loving, promise-keeping Lord, Creator of all things new.

---

[6] Philippians 2:10; Revelation 11:15.

Until that day, we press on! Arrival at our destination is guaranteed:

> We have a building from God, a house not made with hands, eternal in the heavens ... He who has prepared us for this very thing is God, who has given us the Spirit as a guarantee.
> (2 Corinthians 5:1, 5)

As we travel, we actually hear that we have in a very real sense already arrived! Our lives are even now 'hidden with Christ in God' (Colossians 3:3). Could there be any greater security for pilgrims travelling through a dangerous world? Though we often struggle to take another step, we know now that we have 'a safety equal to the treasure; "with Christ in God", a double rampart, all divine.'[7]

Responding

The pilgrimage began in a far-off country, but arrival at our destination is certain, despite the hardships of the journey. Then we will stand with hands raised in worship and blessing in the presence of our Lord. Until that time, we respond and pray with our fellow pilgrims:

> May the covenant, promise-keeping Lord bless us
> and guard us with His protection and love.
> May we know His goodness accompanying us
> along every path we walk.

---

[7] H. C. G.Moule, *Colossian Studies* (London 1898), p.190, quoted by F. F. Bruce, *Commentary on the Epistles to the Ephesians and Colossians* (Grand Rapids, MI: William B Eerdmans Publishing Co., 1957), p261.

May we know the wonder of His grace set on us
before the foundation of the world.
May we know the light of His glorious presence
each day of our wilderness wandering.
May we know His peace both in this dark world
and in the dazzling dawn of eternity.
Lord, keep us faithful on this journey till
we stand in worship and adoring love
before the risen, ascended and glorified Lord Jesus.
Amen.

Postscript

The journey is over. Sore feet and weary limbs are forgotten as we are greeted by the risen Lord of lords and King of kings and led into the presence of His Father. Thrilled beyond measure, all we can do is echo the words of Jude:

> Now to him who is able to keep you from falling, and to make you stand without blemish in the presence of his glory with rejoicing, to the only God our Saviour, through Jesus Christ our Lord, be glory, majesty, power, and authority, before all time and now and for ever. Amen.
> (Jude 1:24-25)

And as we pray, wonder of wonders, we see our risen Lord's scarred hands raised in welcome, blessing us with love that cannot be measured.